COPYRIGHT © BY BILL R. THOMAS

ALL RIGHTS RESERVE

LIBRARY OF CONGRESS CATALOG CARD NUMBER

PRINTED IN THE UNITED STATES OF AMERICA

TO MY CHILDREN – MICHAEL, KENNETH, AND ANGELIQUE
AND TO MY SWEET GRANDDAUGHTERS - CAROLINA
ANGELIQUE, JACQUELINE LEE, & OLIVIA

ALL OF WHOM I LOVE DEEPLY

A WILD SHOT IN THE DARK

INTRODUCTION

I was a "depression" baby (born 1931) and grew up poor in a small town in West Kentucky – Dawson Springs. This story of my childhood and growing up is written for my granddaughters so they will know something about their ancestors - especially "Papa Bear".

Life is really what you make of it. Considering where I began and what I had to work with – I think I did Ok. To the best of my knowledge, me and two first cousins were the first college graduates of the clan. I have had a full life and enjoyed every minute of it – save one or two.

I'm writing this at the ripe old age of 80. I've been married to the same ole gal – Caro – for over 50 years and we have 3 wonderful children, Michael, Kenneth, and Angelique, and three very special granddaughters, Carolina, Jacqueline, and Olivia.

And let's get one thing straight right now – my mother gave me the name Billy Ray – and I never cared for it. I have gone through life as Bill R. or just plain ole Bill.

As I wrote this, one thing became obvious to me. The "Good Ole Days" are definitely the days of your youth. Those are the days you best remember. So parents, do everything in your power to make life pleasant for your children, especially from birth to high school.

This is the first of a two book autobiography. The next book entitled *The Debits Are On The Left; The Credits Are By The Window* covers my accounting career up to the present.

Bill Thomas

TABLE OF CONTENTS

Chapter		Page(s)
1	Ancestors – Coal Miners and Inventors? Not Likely	1
1a	The Family Tree of Bill Thomas	9
2	My Earliest Memories (I Think)	12
3	Orange's Store	24
4	Entertainment That I Remember (Before TV)	28
5	Family Reunions	40
6	Summer at Pa Thomas' Farm	51
7	Summer at Uncle Pate's Farm	62
8	Summer at Uncle Calvin's Farm	78
9	Visits To Other Kin Folks	86
10	Down Into The Bowels Of The Earth	91
11	Help Wanted – Or Vice Versa	96
12	The Four Musketeers	121
13	Our First Car – Model A Ford	136
Pictures	Pictures and Stuff - Descriptions	145
14	Be Prepared	159
15	The First Canadian Boy Scout Jamboree	161
16	December 7, 1941	166

TABLE OF CONTENTS - Continued

Chapter		Page(s)
17	The War Years	173
18	Sports	178
19	A Trip Through Dixie	188
20	Miscellaneous Memories	193
21	What You Got To Swap?	210
22	More Hunting And Fishing	231
23	Zipping Through High School	235
24	Early Courting	239
25	Building Chevrolets	244
26	Go Wildcats!	251
27	Decisions, Decisions, Decisions	268
28	Off We Go – Into The Wild Blue Yonder	281

CHAPTER 1

ANCESTORS – COAL MINERS AND INVENTORS(?) – NOT LIKELY

When I restarted my professional (CPA) career, after service in the Air Force, I felt awfully important. However, when I received my first job review in Texas, my boss, a cantankerous old fossil, told me, "Thomas, you are like a grain of sand in the Sahara desert – the wind could blow you away and no one would notice."

I've thought about that many times and taken in a statistical light, I do in fact represent only appx. 1/7 billionth of the Earth's population. (About like a drop of water in the Pacific Ocean). On the other hand, I know that each of us is <u>unique</u> and very important to someone (family, friends, etc.).

I also firmly believe that everyone's life story could make a very interesting book - some more interesting than others of course. So here goes my autobiography – from my earliest memory until military service. There is a following book which completes my autobiography - *The Debits Are On The Left; The Credits Are By The Window.*

No one knows for sure how humans began. From a religious point of view – it would be when God created Adam and Eve. Or, if you are more of the scientific bent and believe ole Charlie Darwin, you may think you started after a hairy, bow legged, male ape like creature crawled into a cave already occupied by a hairy, bow legged female ape. Before the night was over they had a romantic encounter and he fired a "Wild Shot In The

Dark" which she captured and months later dropped a baby ape on planet Earth.

This process has been repeated millions of times since, - until, in mid March, 1931, the shot was fired that created me. At about that time, several other historic events were taking place on the planet, including:

* The first Mickey Mouse comic strip appeared
* Scotch tape hits the market
* The Planet Pluto was discovered (by Clyde Tombaugh)
* Birdseye frozen food hits the market, and Twinkies were invented
* The country is mired in a depression - a very serious depression
* The first night baseball game was played (Independence, Kansas)
* Mohandas Gandhi was stirring up trouble for the British in India
* Herbert Hoover was President - construction started on Hoover Dam

When I was in high school, one of my classes had an assignment to track our "family tree" as far back as we could. Through my parents and relatives, I was only able to track back about 4 generations. My fraternal side ancestors (Thomas) were originally coal miners from Wales while my maternal side (Bell) were farmers and railroaders from Scotland. My Mother's relatives always claimed they were descendants of Alexander Graham Bell. However, I never could prove it - neither could they. Generally speaking, my ancestors were from the British Isles.

One thing you find out about looking up your ancestors - particularly if you are several generations removed from those that crossed the ocean to settle in America, there is a real <u>duke's mixture</u> of them. In my case, Irish, German, Indian, English, and Dutch. They mostly came from the British Isles to the East Coast of America and migrated inland through the Cumberland Gap. Some were indentured servants that came across the southern states - Alabama, Georgia, etc. They are now scattered mostly throughout the South and Southwest. I realized we were all sort of like mongrel dogs, a mixture of almost everything imaginable, not a pure bred in the bunch.

In capsule form, I grew up in Kentucky, graduated from U.K., put in my military obligation in the Air Force, married a Texan, raised 3 children and spent the rest of my life in Texas, earning my livelihood as a C.P.A.

My dad, Otto Elehue Thomas, was born in Denver, Colorado in 1904. My granddad, Lilbourn Elehue Thomas, had taken his family on a big circle after the Civil War, from Kentucky to Waco, Texas, to Denver, and then back to West Kentucky where they settled on a tobacco farm in Caldwell County and raised a family of ten (yes - 10) (and you think you have cousins!). My dad only completed the eighth grade all a one room school house in Macedonia, Caldwell County, Kentucky. Dad left the farm at an early age and found a job in the coal fields of Southern, Illinois. Later, he moved to Harvey, Illinois (Chicago suburb) and worked in a factory that manufactured heavy duty coal mining equipment. He must have gotten homesick (actually, the factory closed) and drove back to West Kentucky (in a new Model A Ford). He got a Government job at the Veterans Administrations Hospital, near Dawson Springs. He met and married Mom in 1929, just before the "crash" (Depression).

My mom, Edith Lurlene Bell, was born in Kuttawa, Kentucky. She had two brothers and a sister. Her Mother, Pernice Simmons died giving birth to her youngest brother, Tracy, who also died. Mom ended up raising her younger brother, Fratis (Pate), and younger sister, Ouida (Beadie). Mom graduated from high school in Dawson Springs. My granddad, Lynn Boyd Bell (Papa Bell), worked for the railroad and had moved from Lilbourn, Missouri to Kuttawa, Kentucky, and later to Dawson Springs. He got tuberculosis and ended up in a hospital in Chicago for many years. Later, he spent his remaining years living part time with Uncle Fratis' (Pate) family and part time with us. Ouida (Beadie) lived with us until she got married to my cousin Arvil Beshear (dad's sister's son). Beadie then became cousin Beadie, as well as Aunt Beadie.

It goes without saying - we were poor, but so was everyone else we associated with, so you never noticed. We lived in rent houses and Dad had to sell his Model A and he didn't own another car until 1943. He rode the bus to work.

Later, he bought old run down houses and fixed them up and sold them. It seemed like we moved every year. That gives you a little bit of background up to the day I was born, December 19, 1931.

THE FAMILY TREE OF

BILL R. THOMAS

Time Period				
2011	Bill R. Thomas 12/19/31 → Born - Dawson Springs, KY			
1904	Otto E. Thomas 11/26/44 → 8/13/91 Born - Denver, CO		Edith Lurlene Bell 3/19/09 → 8/10/98 Born - Kuttawa, KY	
1870	Lilbourne E. Thomas 8/8/1875 → 4/27/69	Matilda Jane Mitchell 9/4/1879 → 12/3/1963	Lynn Boyd Bell 2/11/1887 → 8/9/1954	Nora Love Simmons 12/1/1891 → 2/18/1921
	See next page (A-1)	(A-2)	(A-3)	(A-4)

THE FAMILY TREE OF

BILL R. THOMAS
(Continued)

Time
Period

A-1

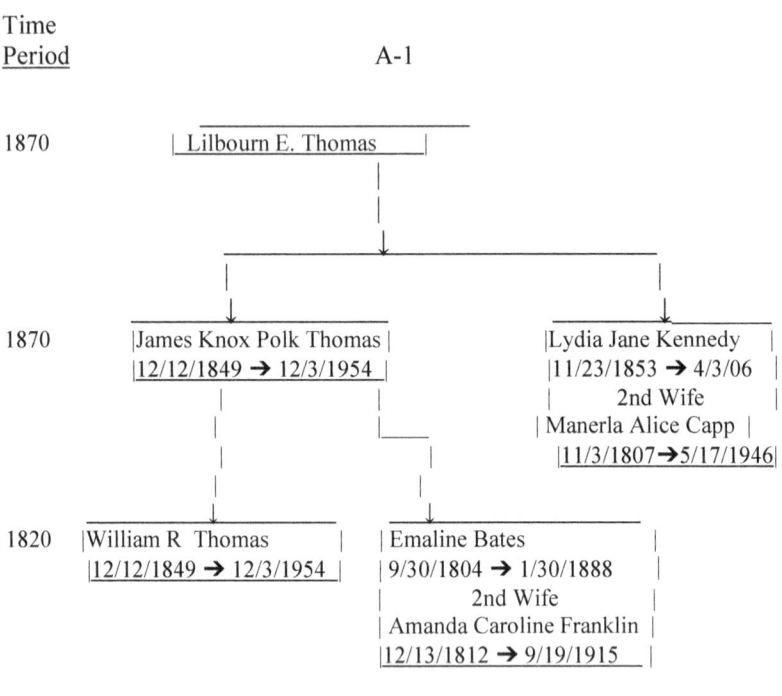

1870 — Lilbourn E. Thomas

1870 — James Knox Polk Thomas | 12/12/1849 → 12/3/1954
Lydia Jane Kennedy | 11/23/1853 → 4/3/06
2nd Wife
Manerla Alice Capp | 11/3/1807 → 5/17/1946

1820 — William R Thomas | 12/12/1849 → 12/3/1954
Emaline Bates | 9/30/1804 → 1/30/1888
2nd Wife
Amanda Caroline Franklin | 12/13/1812 → 9/19/1915

A-2

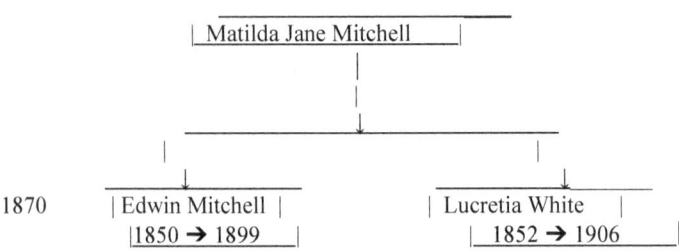

Matilda Jane Mitchell

1870 — Edwin Mitchell | 1850 → 1899
Lucretia White | 1852 → 1906

THE FAMILY TREE OF
BILL R. THOMAS
(Continued)

Time Period

A-3

1870 — Lynn Boyd Bell

1840 — Richard C. Bell 5/2/1837 → 2/18/1889 | Pernecia Calvina Downs 9/29/1856 → 6/9/1940

A-4

1870 — Nora Love Simmons

1840 — William Jefferson Simmons 2/20/1869 → 7/14/1955 | Cora Della Rice Stone 11/4/1870 → 1/10/1947

1860 — Valentine Simmons 5/11/1817 → 2/19/1920 | Macy G. Burnett 5/1/1817 → 6/6/1936 | William Turner Stone 11/25/1834 → 3/14/1923 | Nancy Elizabeth Winfield 3/22/1840 → 7/15/1872

CHAPTER 2

MY EARLIEST MEMORIES (I THINK)

I'm not certain that I actually remember some of the things I'm about to tell you, or whether, I just remember Mom and others telling me about them. It really doesn't make any difference, does it?

<u>Pre School</u>

We lived next door to the Steven's – ma and pa. I use to wake-up early and go to their house and eat breakfast with them, before my parents woke up. I have always been an early riser. Their son, Paul, was my basketball coach later in life.

I was a bed wetter. I remember how cold the wet spots would get in the winter time when I would roll back into them. I also remember my Mom bathing me in a galvanized wash tub which was placed on the floor in the kitchen by the stove.

My hair was light blonde until I was about 12. Some called me "cotton top." My dad use to cut my hair. He was a "self taught" barber and picked up a little change cutting the neighbors hair.

My sister, Loretta, and me use to fight a lot. I usually got the spanking if one was administered. My dad always used his razor strap. It made a lot of noise and hurt like the blazes.

<u>Early School Days</u>

I remember my first grade teacher - Miss Mary Jane Orr. She was tall and wore her hair in a knot. Her brother built an airplane - and flew it over Dawson.

My second grade teacher was Miss Emma Katherine Meadows - I fell in love with her. She spoiled me in school. My second love was a little blonde headed girl in class named Barbara Joyce Robertson. Her family left Dawson and I never knew what happened to her.

My third grade teacher was Miss Evelyn Kesterson, a neighbor. She use to brag on me to the neighbors. I always made straight A's on my report cards.

Fourth grade was Miss Ethel Cox, an Indian, really. She taught me the love of nature and natural things.

It is amazing how much influence your teachers, particularly the first four or five years of school, have upon your life. All of those mentioned stressed reading and I became an avid reader - and remain so to this day. I also remember how my Mother kept stressing to me "You've got to get a good education!"

The thing that I developed a liking for very early in my education was reading. I read everything I could lay my hands on - particularly history. I always wished that I had been born during the days of the western frontier. I would have gone west and built myself a big ranching empire or at least that is what I dreamed.

Dawson had two school buildings, the high school building on the east side of town and the grade school on the south side. The grade school was much newer and had the gymnasium. We lived a block from the high school - which had grades 1,2, & 3 and 9 through 12, but over a mile from the grade school - which had grades 4 through 8. Mr. Rupert A. Belt was the superintendant and Mr. B.U. Sisk was the Principal.

Dawson Springs was and is a small town of about 2,000 folks, and is located in Hopkins County in Western Kentucky. The Tradewater river runs along the west side of town, the Illinois Central Railroad runs East/West through the southern third of town and highway 62 also runs East/West through the middle of town. Dawson is in the corner of Hopkins County near two other counties, Caldwell and Christian. The present governor of Kentucky, Steve Beshears, is from Dawson Springs.

School Plays and Programs

The earliest school program I remember is one in which my sister and I portrayed a dutch boy and girl. My Mother and Aunt Beadie sewed our costumes and ordered authentic wooden shoes for us, which I still have. We got up on stage in our costumes and performed a song and dance.

Getting to school

There was no public transportation in Dawson, or any school buses, except the one to transport the basketball team. So we walked (or ran) to school - remember, we had no car.

Playing after school

The Ashby family lived across the street from us - Doris, Joyce, and Allen (Spud). Joyce was in my grade and Allen in my sister's grade. Joyce could run like a deer and she and I usually raced to and from school. She won about half the time.

Other kids in the neighborhood were Ruth and Charles Sisk (B.U.'s kids), Don and Jack Talley, and Tom Hopkins. We use to play hide-and-seek, tag, red rover, and cowboys and indians. In the Winter when it snowed we built snowmen, had snow ball fights, and made snow cream (snow, milk, sugar, and vanilla flavoring).

We lived within a block of the edge of town and beyond town were fields and woods. Tom Hopkins and I used to trap rabbits in the fields and go hunting with bb guns - sometimes Spud went with us. We built our rabbit traps from scrap lumber we found.

In the Spring when it rained a lot and backwater from the overflowing Tradewater river covered the lower part of the fields, we would catch crayfish (tie a piece of bacon on a string and drop it into their hole - they would grab the bacon with their claws and we would pull them out - they never let go of the bacon). We would build a fire and boil the trails in a can and eat them. Very good eating, ask any Cajun.

Dad sometimes raised a pig (hog) in a pen down in the field behind the school and I would go feed it, most of the time.

The Fugates lived next to the Ashby's. R.B. and Laura were out of school. R.B. ran the movie projector at the local theater (Strand). He was a good story teller (usually movies he had seen). Many a summer night all the neighborhood gang would collect under the street light on Keigan street and R.B. would entertain with stories while Laura fed us stale popcorn, which R.B. had brought from the theater.

The Talley boys got a set of boxing gloves for Christmas and their dad built a makeshift ring in their yard. He gave all the neighborhood boys boxing lessons. Don Talley was my age and he and I would "spar." it usually ended in a slugfest and I usually whipped him, but when I did, brother Jack, who was a couple of years older and about 30 pounds heavier, would take the gloves from Don and and climb into the ring with me and whip my butt. I finally quit boxing them.

Hobos and mad dogs

My Mother always told us to watch out for Hobo's and mad dogs - to come running home if we saw either. A hobo was supposed to be a man in dirty, raggedy clothes, who would be "bumming" for food and money. A mad dog was a stray dog that would be foaming at the mouth. I saw both.

The first hobo was at the back door of a neighbors house, I rushed home and told mom. We peeped out the window and saw him coming toward our house. Soon there was a a knocking at the back door, "anybody home?" My Mother went to the door and opened it. He removed his cap and very politely said, "Maam, I'm from Iowa and I lost my farm and can't find work. Could you spare something to eat." Mom asked, "Do you have a family? What's your name?" He said, "Yes maam, got a wife and 3 kids. They are out at Hooverville waiting for me. My name is Leonard Hamilton." Mom said, "Just a minute and she went to the kitchen while I just stood and watched Leonard. He finally asked "Boy, do you think you could get me some coffee or water - anything to drink?" I went to the kitchen and told Mom and she poured a mug of coffee and I carried it to him. He gulped it down. Soon Mom returned with a bag full of food – cold biscuits, jars of vegetables she had canned (corn, green beans, beets, blackberry jelly), some pet milk, and a packet of salt. He took the food and with tears in his eyes thanked her and asked God to bless her.

After he left I asked "Where is "Hooverville?" She sat me down and explained the "Depression" to me as best she could. She said it was caused by President Hoover. "Hoboes" were people men mostly, broke and out of work, who hitched rides on freight trains and rode all over the country, looking for work and begging for food. She said if my Dad didn't have the Government job, we could be hoboes ourselves.

Then she stressed the golden rule "Do unto others as you would have them do unto you."

After that, many, many, many hoboes knocked on our back door and my Mother always fed them, although at the time we had to skip a meal or two because of it.

Mad Dogs

One day we were out playing and I heard my sister scream and saw her running toward home. I took out after her. Mother met us at the door and said, "What's the matter?" Sis said, "Mad Dog," - and pointed toward the Ashby's. A brown looking dog with slobber hanging out his mouth was standing out in the middle of the street. Poochie, our dog, was napping under the house, but came charging out, barking and growling. I threw open the door and ran to catch him, screaming, "Poochie, stop! Come back here!" Thank heaven, Poochie stopped and I caught him and was holding him tightly as the Dawson Police car came to a screeching stop in front of the house. Police Chief, Wild Bill Boutcher, jumped out, pistol drawn, and started shooting at the "Mad Dog" as he advanced toward it. He finally hit it with about his fourth shot, then walked up to it and shot it again. He drug it to the car and put it in the trunk and left.

The next day's paper (Dawson Progress) had an article about the incident and said the dogs head had been sent to Madisonville and they confirmed that it was indeed rabid.

CHAPTER 3

ORANGES' STORE

Back in the olden days, as my granddaughter Carolina described them we had the first "convenience stores" but we didn't describe them as such. We called them "neighborhood grocery stores." The one in our neighborhood (Keigan Street in east Dawson) was "Orange's Store." Later, Mr. Orange died and the store was bought by Mrs. Bertha Lancaster, Doug's grandmother, and it became "Lancaster's Store."

The store carried bread, milk, canned goods, potatoes, beans, flour, meal, salt, sugar, bologna, cheese, crackers, eggs, thimbles, needles, kerosene, candy, etc.

Although milk was delivered door to door, in bottles by horse and buggy, sometime we would run out. One day my Mom sent me to the store to get a pound of soup beans (Great Northern Beans) and a quart of milk. She gave me a quarter and told me I could also buy two 1¢ BB bats suckers - 1 for me and 1 for Sis.

Our pet, a small French Bulldog named Poochie, followed me to the store. Poochie was famous for two things, both starting with F. He would try to romance every female dog he met, and he would fight every male dog he met.

As I approached Orange's store from the East, Poochie at my heels, Kenneth Alexander, with his large German Shepherd at his heels, was approaching from the West. I arrived first, made my purchases, and Mr. Orange put them in a big paper bag and I started to leave. I met Kenneth at the door and a terrible dog fight erupted on the porch. By the time I got outside, Kenneth's dog had

Poochie by the throat and pinned down on the porch, literally choking the life out of him. I yelled for Kenneth to pull his dog off poor little ole Poochie. Kenneth just stood in the door laughing. I looked for a weapon and all I saw was my sack of groceries which I had set down on the porch. I rushed to it and retrieved the quart of milk (a bottle). Then I rushed into the middle of the dog fight and hit the big German Shepherd on the head with the bottle, which broke, scattered glass, and splashed milk all over the porch. Kenneth's big dog rolled over on his back, tongue hanging out, eyes closed. I thought I had killed him. Poochie got up, shook himself, and trotted off toward home.

About that time, Kenneth walloped me on the side of the head with his fist and I spun around and we squared off. Since I had been boxing the Talley boys, I knew a little about boxing and was getting the best of it. Mr. Orange came out. He broke up the fight, and got a broom and dust pan and made me clean up the mess. Kenneth's dog woke up and Kenneth led him off, threatening to get even with me every step he took.

When I got home and told Mom what happened, she scolded me and threatened to give Poochie away because he was a "trouble maker." I pleaded for him and locked him in the shed and went back to the store to get another bottle of milk.

Years later I had another fight on that porch.

CHAPTER 4

ENTERTAINMENT THAT I REMEBER (Before TV)

I remember many grownups discussing what a "hick town" Dawson Springs was, especially my Mother. They always said it was "drying up." Maybe it was. As I grew older and learned something of its history, then it truly had long since passed its peak.

At around the turn of the Century (1900) or there abouts, Dawson Springs, Kentucky was a tourist attraction, the primary attraction being its mineral water (a miniature "Hot Springs"). After the Illinois Central Railroad came right through the small community in west Kentucky and the mineral water was discovered, tourism was promoted and folks started arriving by the train load. Several hotels were built, the largest and most famous being The New Century Hotel. Bath houses were built, i.e. The Hamby Well. A park and boat rides were provided on the Tradewater River at the Mill Dam. Tourist were also entertained by a semi pro baseball team. Old timers swore that the population of Dawson in those good ole days grew to at least 25,000 during the peak of tourist season. Who knows?

By the way, Dawson Springs was named for the fellow who gave the land for the rail line right of way and depot - Bryant N. Dawson.

Later, the coal mining industry took over the economy and the era of tourism ended Dawson's population was around 2,000.

But for a young boy growing up in the 1930's, Dawson Springs was paradise. In addition to school and playing with kids in the neighborhood, I remember the following forms of entertainment - at least what I called entertainment:

   *Hiking and picnics
   *Fishing and swimming
   *Radio programs
   *Movies
   *Family reunions
   *Tent meetings
   *Popcorn and cards
   *Bisbee comedians
   *Circus/carnivals
   *Visiting relatives

Hiking and picnics and fishing and swimming

Remember, we didn't have a car and there was no public transportation, so when we went anywhere, we walked. In the summertime, Mom would sometimes prepare a picnic basket after church on Sunday and we would hike out into the country for a picnic. Our usual destination were either the abandoned C.C.C. Camp (it had a picnic table), Rosedale Cemetery (resting place of many relatives), or the State Park (it had a lake - and we went swimming).

C.C.C. was the Civilian Construction Corp, one of the means The Roosevelt Democrats used to try to break the vice grip of the depression and put America back to work. They built a "camp" at Dawson and the workers built the State Park, Pennyrile Park, and Rosedale Cemetery, in and around Dawson.

There were several other things that happened about that time which were a part of what the adults described as Roosevelt's "New Deal." I would hear my parents, neighbors, and relatives discussing, actually arguing, about them.

First, there was the "Resettlement." The Federal Government bought up a bunch of old poor farms, moved the families off of them, built a big lake, and created the

Pennyrile Park and Forest (They planted many pine trees).

Next was the WPA (Works Project Administration). The Federal Government hired men and put them to work building stuff.

Finally, the Government went around the farms buying livestock, killed it, burned it, plowed up crops.

Those that approved of the "New Deal" claimed Roosevelt saved the nation and got the economy back in gear.

Those opposed said he was a dictator and destroyed food while folks starved, uprooted families from the land, etc.

I was too young to have any strong feelings, one way or another.

Radio Programs

There were a few radio programs that the family listened to regularly, just like you watch certain T.V. programs today. Our family favorites were:

*Fibber McGee & Molly
*Lum & Abner
*Jack Benny
*The Grand Ole Opry

Movies

There was a theater in Dawson - the "Strand." It was owned by "Pat" Meadows and our neighbor, R.B. Fugate, operated the projectors. Bill Kittinger popped and sold popcorn. Whenever I could save up the 11¢ for admission, I would go to the Saturday afternoon matinee. It was always a double feature, a western and usually a mystery, plus cartoons and a cereal. My favorite star was Tom Mix, and his horse Tony, Jr.

Tent Meetings

I don't mean this to be disrespectful - just stating fact. The Holiness Church (Pentecostal) tent meetings which were "revivals" in the summer were entertaining. They were held in a large tent and the walls (sides) were rolled up to let the air inside, otherwise the heat would have been unbearable.

By rolling up the sides, the meeting were truly "open to the public." The Preachers were loud as was the music and lively.

But the real entertainment came from the faith healing and speaking in the unknown tongue. I witnessed many a miracle - folks on crutches who would throw them away and run up and down the aisle yelling what sounded like - kchitty - kchitty - kchitty. Others would wallow around on the ground, while others would climb the tent poles, all the time marking very strange noises.

Popcorn and Cards

My Dad was an excellent card player. He taught Loretta and I many card games - poker, pitch, rook, cribbage, solitaire, and bridge. We spent many a long winter evening playing cards. Our favorite game was Rook. Most of the time some of the neighbors would come over and we would have Rook tournaments. You drew cards for partners and 4 players would play on the kitchen table while the others would either stand around and watch or sit in the living room and visit and listen to the radio.

My sister or me, whoever wasn't playing, would start popping popcorn and serving it to the guests. We had a corn popper that you held over the fire in the grate (our house was heated by a coal fire in grates, (fireplaces in each room) and shook the corn popper when the corn started popping. The drink was usually Kool-aid or Lemon-aide.

Later, one of the neighbors, I think it was Les Schwab, gave us an electric popcorn popper. My parents used it till they passed away.

Dad and whoever his partner was won the tournaments at least 90% of the time.

I still enjoy playing cards - ask my granddaughters.

Bisbee Comedians

I saved the best for last. The epitome of entertainment in my memory was a Kentucky Chautauqua called Bisbee Comedians. This was a tent show which usually came to Dawson every summer. It featured Toby and Susie. It had many skits - Toby usually played a freckle faced country bumpkin and Susie, his snaggle toothed girlfriend. Most skits pitied these two, who were in real life husband and wife - Leo and Dawn Larsen, against city slickers who were always trying to fleece them.

Circus/Carnivals

Every year or so a circus or carnival would come through Dawson for a night or so. Some came by rail and some by truck. Either way, all the boys in Dawson gathered around to help unload, set up the tent, feed the animals, etc. We didn't get paid but were given free passes, which we sold at discounted prices.

The thing I remember most were the Circus - The Big Elephants and their act and the clowns, and the Carnival - the rides - Ferris wheel, swings, tilt a whirl, etc.

I remember one carnival side show that had a sheep man, and the man had sheep wool all over his chest, back, face, and head. I always wondered. I wasted many nickels trying to knock the bottles over with a baseball.

Oh, I also remember a carnival that had a prize fighter and they offered $20 to anyone who could go three, three minute rounds with him. Uncle Calvin took them up on it and climbed into the ring with a professional prize fighter and knocked him out within 30 seconds (Calvin learned to box in the Navy and was champion of something).

Today's movies and television don't come close to matching the quality of the live entertainment I experienced in my youth.

Visiting Relatives

Most of my Dad's folks lived in and around Dawson and the families visited one another frequently. Most visits ended with popcorn popping and card playing, particularly Rook. However, the visits I remember most were those overnight stays and multiple day visits to some of my favorites and the food that Ma Thomas prepared was delicious. There was always a couple of meat dishes, many vegetables, biscuits and cornbread, and pies and cakes. They were poor but we ate like royalty. I loved pickled beets and she served them to me every meal, including breakfast.

CHAPTER 5

FAMILY REUNIONS

Every year the Thomas clan had a family reunion. We would meet at Pa Thomas' (my granddad) farm on his birthday, August 8th. My great grandfather, James Knox Polk Thomas, was always there along with about a hundred uncles, aunts, and cousins.

I always looked forward to this fun day. It was exciting to visit with my cousins and pitch horseshoes or washers, play croquet, sometimes fish in the pond or ride horses, and of course, eat till we popped. Each of the women brought food and they tried to outdo each other - chicken, hams, casseroles, breads, many vegetables, pies, cakes, candy, and of course, "homemade ice cream".

Usually the kids started turning the cranks on the ice cream freezers but when it became too hard to crank, an uncle would take over and finish the job.

There were also family reunions on my Mother's side, but they were held at my great grandfathers farm near Fairview, KY, about 45 miles away. I only remember going to one of them. One year my Uncle Pate bought a used Ford pickup truck and we all loaded up in the bed of it and went to the W.J. Simmons Plantation. Old WJ, was my Mothers', Mothers' Father (mom's grandfather in other words. He was the only one in my "family" in those days who "had money" as my Mother used to say in fact, he was very wealthy - owned about 1,000 acres of black land, a bank, a stave factory (used in making barrels) in Hopkinsville, and part interest in a tobacco warehouse. They say he made his money from slave labor - his children. He was a mean old soul and cussed like a sailor.

Still Fighting the Civil War

Great grandfather W.J. Simmons did not appear to be fond of the Thomas'. I asked my Mother about this. Mom said, "Don't pay any attention to that, my granddad Simmons is still fighting the Civil War." I asked her to explain. She explained that Kentucky was a border state in the war and its citizens were split in their loyalties, some siding with the north and some with the south. Old W.J. was a confederate to the bone and was a friend of Jefferson Davis who was from Fairview, Kentucky, about 50 miles from where W.J. lived. W.J. had been a Colonel in Jeb Stuarts Cavalry. Seven from the Thomas clan had gone across the Ohio River and joined the union Army in Illinois. W.J. never forgot that and never approved of his granddaughter's marriage to a damn Yankee.

Mom said, the Ku Klux Klan burned the cross in their yard right after she married my dad. She had no proof but always thought old W.J. had something to to do with it.

I remember listening to many adults "fighting" the Civil War as I was growing up.

I'll never forget that weekend. It was a storybook weekend for me. The old Ford pickup was straining with its over load, the Bell family and our family plus Beadie, for a total of 9. It seemed like it took a half a day to go from Dawson to Fairview. We stopped often to add water to the radiator and let it cool off.

When we finally got there we turned down this long tree lined drive that ended at a large white antebellum southern mansion, complete with the large columns. (Later in life when I viewed *"Gone With The Wind"* I thought, the house looks like Papaw Simmons place). When we stopped, the large yard filled with kin folks I had never seen before, and some never since. All day long I kept tugging on Mama's skirt and pointed out people, mostly second cousins, and asking "Who is that?" My Mother would tell me and then scold me for not remembering their names and for pointing. Before the day was over I was calling all the adult males "Uncle," the females "Aunt," and the children "cousin."

The one thing in common with the Thomas reunion was the food. There was enough to feed an army - and all of it delicious.

One of my cousins, Tinsie, kind of took a shine to me (and me to her), and she offered to give me a tour of the mansion. It had huge double front doors that opened into the largest room I had ever seen - 2 stories to the ceiling and a large fireplace in one end, there was a spiral stair case to the second floor level - and I lost count of the rooms - probably about 20. The kitchen contained the largest cook stove I had ever seen. The dining room had the largest and longest table I had ever seen. There were two Negros, as Tinsie called them, in the kitchen - large buxomed and jolly. They did the cooking and housework. We ended up in the attic where Tinsie showed me something that few were privileged to see - W.J.'s Civil War uniform and saber. He had been a colonel in the Confederate Cavalry. In the same trunk was his revolver, belt, scabbard, and a leather bag with a draw string on it. Tinsie loosened it and showed me the gold coins - more money than I thought existed in the whole world. I was awe struck with all I had seen Tinsie finally said, "We better get out of here before Papa catches us. He'll whup you if he does." I asked if he whupped her. She said, "No, I'm his favorite grandchild" (and obviously she was - for the devil himself was standing in the doorway and had us trapped). Old W.J. shouted, "Tinsie, what in heck are you doing in here. You know you ain't supposed to come in here. And who is this little tow headed boy?" I reared back and said, "I'm Bill Thomas, by gawd," as strongly as I could. He said "I ought to turn you across my knee and whup your butt." I said, "You and who else you old fart?"

He reared back and laughed and said to Tinsie "This little fart must be kin of mine, he's got spunk. Who's boy is he anyway?" Tinsie said, "He's Aunt Edith's son, from Dawson Springs." He looked me over good and said

"Fine, fine," Tinsie and I slipped out the door, flew down the stairs, and went outside. Tinsie said, "Let's go to the barn, there's something else I want to show you." We went inside the barn and there sat a brand spanking new Model T Ford car, on blocks. Tinsie said W.J. bought it and had it delivered, but never learned how to drive. He wouldn't let any of his sons drive it either. They drove wagons instead.

That night when we piled into that battered old Ford truck, it would not start. Uncle Pate ran the battery down trying to start it. No go. My great grandmother Simmons insisted that we spend the night, so we did. There was plenty of room, but a shortage of beds, so my cousins (Jimmy and Glen), my sister, and myself slept on pallets on the floor.

I'll never forget the wakeup call the next morning. There was an extremely loud and vibrating "BANG! BANG! BANG!," followed by "Get up god dang it. Daylights a burning, get ready for work!" "BANG." We crawled to the railing and peeped over to the floor below. There stood old W.J. next to a large Bell mounted on a frame, with a hammer in his hand, all drawn back and ready to whack it one more time. Bear in mind, this was <u>Sunday</u> morning.

By the time we got dressed and down to the dining table, everyone was there but us. They were already eating, but there was still lots of ham, sausage, biscuits, gravy, etc., in platters and serving dishes. As we ate, W.J. was barking out the orders for the day. Uncle Ellis was to take Uncle Pate into town to get the battery charged and bring back a mechanic to fix the old truck.

W.J. planned to start cutting tobacco that day and hanging it in the barn to cure. He looked me right in the eye and asked, "Can you drive a team of mules?" I said, "Yes sir." He said, "Good, you can haul tobacco to the barn," and I did all day long. The team was hitched to a sled and I drove to the tobacco field where the tobacco was loaded and then to the barn where it was unloaded. We stopped at noon for lunch, then back to work. There was no doubt the Simmons were hard workers. Even old W.J. who cut tobacco all day in the hot sun. At about 5 p.m., Uncle Pate came and got me and said we were leaving, the truck was fixed. I said "Goodbye to all my new found Uncles and they gave me hugs, then "Goodbye to Grandpa. Old W.J. gave me a hug and I felt something in my pocket. We walked back to the truck and I reached in my pocket to check. W.J. had dropped a silver dollar in it. The first dollar I ever earned. The trip home was uneventful but I remember that in the conversations someone mentioned the "Golden Rule." Papa Bell said, W.J.'s version is "Him with the gold rules."

CHAPTER 6

SUMMER AT PA THOMAS' FARM

I always looked forward to the last day of school, starting at about the fourth grade. That meant I could go spend several weeks with my paternal grandparents, Lilbourn (Lib) and Matilda (Tildy) Thomas. Their farm was about ten miles west of Dawson, on the Cadiz Hill Road (dirt) near the Piney Grove Cemetery. The first summer I spent with them (1941), both my Uncle Calvin and Aunt Mildred were still living with them. The next summer both had left. Calvin joined the Navy and Mildred married Uncle Wade.

I slept on a pallet on the floor by a screen door. There was no air conditioning and on some hot muggy nights you would sweat so much that the quilts would get wet and it was hard to fall asleep.

I would awaken in the morning to a BANG! BANG! "Time to get up sleepy heads," as Pa Thomas beat on a dish pan. Ma Thomas would have a huge breakfast prepared – ham, bacon, sausage, biscuits, gravy, grits, milk, butter, and jelly, etc.

After breakfast, I would accompany Calvin to the barn to milk the cows. They usually had six to eight cows, Jersey and Guernsey. After milking, we would carry the milk back to the screened in, back porch. My job then was to run the milk through the DeLeval separator. I can still hear it start to whine as you turned the crank. While I performed this task, Calvin would feed the mules, harness them up, and head for the fields. Mildred would help me clean up the cream separator.

Pa Thomas would put the cream can out by the road where a wagon would come by later and haul it to Princeton. Then he would take the skim milk to the barn, add bran to it, and "slop the hogs."

Next, I would either walk to the field where Calvin was working and help him, or grab a hoe and go to the garden to chop weeds, under the supervision of Aunt Mildred.

Depending on what he was doing, Uncle Calvin would let me help him, usually drive the team of mules, except for plowing. I couldn't handle that. I could handle disking, harrowing, dragging, and cultivating.

At lunch time we would unhitch the mules and ride them back to the farm house. Ma Thomas would have enough food prepared for at least ten people. There were always at least two meats (usually ham and chicken) and corn, potatoes, beans, greens, pickles, beets, cornbread and biscuits, and cake and pie. As we gathered around the table, she always said, "Take a seat and sit down to eat, if you see anything fitten to eat." Then she would apologize because we didn't have any bread. Pa Thomas would always say, "Sit down Tildy. We can make out without store bought bread." He would say grace and we would eat till we almost popped. Then everyone would find a cool spot and take a nap for about one hour, then back to work.

I always prayed for rain. Rain meant, no work, but a squirrel hunt instead.

After we milked and fed the livestock, Calvin would get out his new .22 cal. Remington repeating rifle and a much used .22 cal. Stevens single shot. Guess who got the Stevens. When Calvin joined the Navy, he came by our house and gave me the Stevens and said "If I don't make it back from the war, the Remington is yours. I hugged him and bawled like a baby. Next, he would count out (10) .22 cal. Cartridges and give them to me and we would head for the woods. The woods we went to depended on whatever the squirrels were eating on at the time. If it was beach nuts, we would go to Montgomery Creek. If it was mulberries, we would go across the road and up the hill on the Hale Place (owned by a neighbor). If it was hickory nuts, we would go up the road to Berkley hollow (on the Chambliss Place – owned by the parents of my Uncle Dewey, husband of Dad's sister Cora).

Calvin was a very good marksman and had taught me how to shoot. I wasn't a bad shot, if I say so for myself. Dad always said, "Toot your own horn, otherwise it might not get tooted." When we got to wherever we were going to hunt, we would split up. Calvin was a "still" hunter and would find a tree where there were squirrel signs, pick a spot, and sit down and wait for a squirrel to appear. Then nail him. I was a "stalker." I would slip barefooted through the woods, watching and listening for a squirrel. When I located one I would try to slip up on him. When I got a clear shot, I would take it, but only if I was sure I could hit it, which I usually did.

When I got a squirrel, I would cut a short piece a small tree limb, sharpen both ends of it, punch holes in the rear legs of the squirrel, then run the stick through a belt loop and string him up. This left both hands free so I could shoot another.

Calvin and I We usually stayed within shouting distance of one another and when he was ready to go to the house, he would call me. He usually wasn't ready to quit until he had killed about six squirrels. I would usually have 3 or 4, but sometimes, not often, I would have more on my stringer than him. "When we got back to the house, we would clean the squirrels, put them in a pan of water, and give them to Ma Thomas to cook – fried squirrel, biscuits and gravy for breakfast, and squirrel stew for supper – mighty fine vittles.

After cleaning the squirrels and eating them, we would mend harness, clean out the barn, repair equipment, etc. Sometimes during berry season, Ma Thomas would hand us some buckets and say "If you all would go pick some blackberries, I'll make a cobbler and some jam." You all included Mildred, who would join us. There were many blackberry vines in the pastures, especially along gulley's.

Another ritual occurred on Sundays. We would all get spruced up after breakfast, load up in the buggy and go to church at Piney Grove. Time was spent after church and after hanging around and visiting with neighbors, then we would go home and eat a light lunch of leftover's. Pa Thomas would look at me and say "A mess of fried perch sure would be nice for supper." I would take the hint and after eating I would get a hoe and can and go down by the hog pen to dig up some worms. Then I would get a fishing pole from the side of the smoke house (always 3 or 4 poles there – hanging on long nails), and go down to Montgomery Creek (which ran through the back of the farm) and fish. I caught mostly sun perch (blue gills, etc.) When I had a stringer full, I would go back to the house and clean them.

Before supper, I would build a fire where fires were built to boil clothes, render lard, etc. Mildred would make batter (eggs and buttermilk), drop the fish in it, roll them in corn meal, and put them on a platter. When everything was ready, she would get a big iron skillet and plop a blob of lard into it and put it on the hot coals. When the lard melted and got hot and started popping, she would put the fish into it and cook them.

Supper then was fried fish, pickles, corn on the cob, and lemonade or tea, and cornbread of course. A feast fit for a king (Pa Thomas).

The hardest part of those summers was going back to Dawson when they were over.

P.S.

You might have noticed that I didn't mention Pa Thomas doing any work. He didn't - he said that was what the 10 kids he and Tildy raised was for. A little on the lazy side? Perhaps.

Montgomery Creek ran across the back of the farm and it contained many fish – catfish, perch, pike, bass, carp and buffalo, etc. Pa Thomas loved to eat fish more than anyone I ever knew. At least once on every visit he would say, "Bill, why don't we go down to the creek and catch us a good mess of fish?" And of course, I was always ready. We never failed to catch a sizable stringer of fish. His favorite was perch, which he called "Peerch."

For some reason, I particularly remember helping Ma Thomas with the milk. She would strain it through a cloth and pour it in the cream separator. My job was to turn the crank on the separator. I can still hear the gears singing, the pitch getting higher and higher the faster I turned the crank. I watched the cream come out of one spout and skim milk out the other. The cream was poured into a large metal cream can and was later carried to Princeton and sold to the Princeton Creamery. The skim milk was captured in buckets and later bran was mixed with it and it was fed to the hogs.

I also helped Ma Thomas in her garden, about an acre of every conceivable vegetable and melon. She canned enough to last the year, and much more which she gave to her children.

They also had a big orchard and a grape arbor. I can still taste that wonderful fruit, picked right off the tree, or grapevines.

CHAPTER 7

SUMMER AT UNCLE PATE'S FARM

Uncle Pate (mom's brother) bought a small farm out toward Ilsley (and near Menser School) and a new black Ford pickup. The family gossip was that he "borrowed" the money from papa Bell (my maternal grandfather) who knows? And now "who cares"? Anyway it was about 50 acres he and Papa Bear mostly grew a "truck patch" and raised a few hogs, a horse and a milk cow. Aunt Francis was red headed and my cousins, Jim, Glen (Bubbie), Pat and Sue were likewise carrot tops. Mom had red hair also and dad had jet black hair. By now, my hair had turned to brown. Papa Bell was bald and in the final analysis - his genes prevailed - I too am now bald on top.

Back to the story. The summer at Uncle Pates was strictly a fun summer - all play and no work. There was a shallow pond that we swam in, an old barn where we had corn cob fights, sling shots that Papa Bell made for us, The "Blue Hole" down the road where we fished, and a grapevine in the holler where we would swing.

Jim (Jimmy) was my age and Glen (Bubbie) was almost 2 years younger. (Pat and Susie came along about 10 years later). We used to slip out in the truck patch if no one was watching and each pick a watermelon and take it to the woods. We would find a sharp rock and bust them open and pull out the heart (center) of the melons and eat it. The problem was, the juice was messy and got all over our clothes. The solution was to go jump in the pond, clothes and all, and take a swim. Problem - Bubbie couldn't swim so he would just wade around and get the water muddy. When we would finish and crawl out - the juice was gone but had been replaced by a thin layer of mud. When we would get a little feisty with one another, we would head to the old barn and have a three way corn cob fight. I was a better thrower than either cousin so it usually ended with me against both of them. There was a persimmon tree near the barn and I would slip out, cut a limber limb and sharpen one end of it, gather a pocket full of green persimmons, and start whipping persimmons at them until someone got hit in the head and started crying and running toward the house - war over!

Papa Bell decided to intervene so he made a sling shot for Bubbie. That stopped the corn cob/persimmon wars. After much begging, he made sling shots for Jim and I. We would go hunting with sling shots but shot mostly

English sparrows. One day we were sitting in the front yard under a big maple tree when a dominecker hen walked around the house into the yard - about 100 feet from us. I said "Bubbie, bet you can't hit that chicken." He put a rock in his sling shot, pulled it back, took aim, and let fly. He hit that old hen in the head and she fell over dead. Jim went and told on him and Aunt Francis got mad - at everyone (Papa Bell included because he had made those darn dangerous weapons). She made us clean the chicken and we had chicken and dumplings for supper. A delicious meal I might add.

Papa Bell loved to fish - even more than my Pa Thomas loved to eat fish. I'll always remember the day that we loaded up the Ford pickup with camping and fishing supplies and drove to the Blue Hole for a weekend of fishing. We being - Uncle Pate, Papa Bell, Jim, Bub and myself.

The Blue Hole was near the highway overpass over the railroad - almost three miles from my uncle's farm. It was really the pit that resulted from digging the fill dirt to construct the highway overpass and was probably dug out around 1937 or 1938. It sloped from a shallow end down to a deep end, perhaps fifteen feet deep, and had a bluff running down one side of it. The other side was a woods. The water in the Blue Hole was unusually clear and had a aqua "tinge" to it - most said because there was a copper vein in the rock on the bottom of it. There were cattails, lily pads, and cane growing on the shallow end and scattered trees along the upper end. I would guess that the Blue Hole had about 40 to 50 surface acres. Because of the clearness of the water and the vantage point offered by the bluff, it was a near-perfect classroom to study the mysteries of what went on under the water, I shall never forget its lessons.

If you think ours is a tough environment, you should have seen the things I saw going on in the Blue Hole - snakes eating fish, turtles eating fish, birds eating fish, coons eating fish, fish eating snakes, fish eating bugs, fish eating birds, fish eating fish, etc., etc. (but not fish eating coons). I think they call this the "food chain", but to me, it appeared to be a case of the "big ones" always eating the "little ones" - no chain to it. Some of the lessons I learned in general were:

1. Fishing generally wasn't much good on a clear, bright day - the fish were always in "hiding". (they were really just trying to stay out of the bright sun

rays - just like we were by sitting under a shade tree.)

2. You hardly ever saw a catfish - they stayed in the deepest water and fed at night - except when a train passed! (When a train went by, the vibration started a chain reaction - crawfish, minnows, etc. stated moving; bugs jumped in the water, etc.., and the larger fish took advantage of the situation and them! Only a train or two per day traveled that rail line, however.)

3. The best fishing was generally on a cloudy, overcast day - when it rained, fishing was sometimes the best of all. (The rain apparently dropped the water temperature slightly and added oxygen - thus stimulating activity.)

4. Bass, in particular, seemed to be just downright mean and ornery - the bullies of the "Blue Hole". Most of the time that you got a bait or lure near them, they attacked! Some of the things I observed about bass from the vantage point of the bluff were the following:

* On more than one occasion, I saw red wing blackbirds sitting on a cattail (singing to the bass, as Papa Bell would say) and see a bass jump out of the water, trying to catch them.

* I have observed bass cruising around "wolf pack" style - trying to corner smaller bait fish. (it always seemed that the bass in such packs were of a uniform size - usually 2 or 3 pounders.)

* I have seen frogs leap into the blue water and a bass immediately give pursuit - and usually catch.
* On more than one occasion, I saw redwing blackbirds sitting on a cattail (singing to the bass, as Papa Bell would say) and see a bass jump out of the water, trying to catch them.
* I've seen small snakes swimming across the lake disappear in a big "slurp" as large bass came up out of the deep and almost nonchalantly open their mouths and suck them in.
* I've watched small bass rise to the surface to catch grasshoppers that made the mistake of landing on the water - yet, they made no attempt to catch snake doctors, nickel bugs, etc. (although the stupid little bream would sometimes wear themselves out trying to catch these elusive bugs.)

Mother Nature holds school in the Blue Hole.

* I've seen spawning bass attack everything that got near their "beds." They usually just "slapped" at things and didn't appear to be trying to eat them.

During the bass fishing craze of the '70's and '80's, I read many articles in magazines about most of these observations. I generally smile an inward smile and say to myself - "I knew that - I learned it at the Blue Hole many, many years ago."

Wild grapes were often found in the woods near Uncle Pate's farm. We were always on the lookout for them for two reasons. First the wild grapes were quite tasty and made excellent wine (which Papa Bell was expert at making). And second, you sometimes found one growing up a tree in such a way that you could cut it at ground level and climb the tree and cut the tentacles that attached to the tree trunk and make an excellent swing. (And I almost forgot - you could also smoke grapevine).

We had made several grapevine swings on the farm but the best one was in a holler across the road from the house. One day we were swinging on the grapevine and decided to have a contest. (You may note that we were competitive cousins). The grapevine was on a large hillside tree and the contest was to see who could swing out far enough to grab a hand full of leaves and bring them back to the starting point. At stake were six marbles (we each put 2 in the pot - winner take all).

Bub was first and got within inches but couldn't quite reach the limbs. He complained that we didn't push him hard enough. Next turn was mine and I <u>know</u> they didn't push me hard enough - and told them so. Finally it was Jimbo's (Jimmy was chubby and we called him Jimbo sometimes.) turn. We started pushing him and he kept getting higher and higher and screaming at us to "push harder" - and we did. He finally got high enough to grab a hand full of leaves and "crack" - the grapevine broke and Jim came plunging down. I'll swear he bounced when he hit the ground. We ran down the hill to him and he was out cold - one of his arms was broken and the bone had punched through the skin.

Bub ran to the house to tell Aunt Francis and I stayed with Jimmy. Uncle Pate was at work and there was no transportation available. However, as luck would have it, the mailman came by at that time and they flagged him down and he and Papa Bell came down and got Jimmy and with Bub and my help we carried and drug him to the road and loaded him into the mail carriers Model T. Aunt Francis got in the car and they went racing to Dr. Boitnett's office in Dawson.

Bub and I were scared to death as we waited for their return. Of course, we imagined the worse. Hours later they returned. Jimmy was all bandaged up and had an arm in a sling and a black eye. Aunt Francis explained that Jimmy had a broken collar bone and a broken arm and couldn't play anymore until he got well. She scolded both of us. That night when Uncle Pate returned from work he hauled me back to my home in Dawson.

Bub didn't learn his sling shot lesson however. Later that summer I spent the night with them. The next day we were sitting on the porch, eating a watermelon which we had picked from Papa Bell's watermelon patch, and spotted a yellow cat sneaking through the weeds. Bubbie said to me "I'll bet you a dollar you can't hit that cat." I said "It's a bet" as I laid down the slice of melon and picked up my sling shot. I fumbled in my pocket and selected a rock, placed it in the leather, pulled the rubber strips out - and let fly. I missed but came close enough that the cat jumped and climbed part way up a tree. I looked around at Bub who was loaded and ready to fire - I said "Another dollar" and he nodded and let go. The rock sailed through the air and hit the poor cat in the head

- killing it instantly. Jimmy said "Bubbie, why did you do that, that's Mrs. Vandiver's house cat."

Bubbie jumped up and ran and got a shovel. He and I gave the cat a Christian burial out in the woods. The next day Mrs. Vandiver appeared and asked Aunt Francis if she had seen her missing yellow cat. Aunt Francis, not knowing what had happened, said "no maam." Then, Mrs. Vandiver asked "have you boys seen my cat?"

Bubbie said, "I saw it 4 or 5 days ago down by our barn." Mrs. Vandiver said "No, it was at the house day before yesterday - I mean in the last day or two." "No maam" we chimed in unison. There was silence as she looked us over. I think she was suspicious.

Bubbie spoke again" an owl might of caught her - I heard Arlie Chapel say once that he saw a big owl swoop down and catch one of his cats and fly off with it."

She didn't particularly like that explanation but accepted it and left. RIP old yellow cat.....

Did I pay Bubbie the $2.00. Naw, we always bet "on the cuff" and never paid off. As we grew older the size of our bets grew - sometimes into the millions.

Aunt Francis and Uncle Pate has a "second" family later in life - Pat and Sue.

CHAPTER 8

A SUMMER AT UNCLE CALVIN'S FARM

Within days after the Japanese attacked Pearl Harbor, my Uncle Calvin joined the Navy. After boot camp and training, he was sent to the South Pacific and assigned to the USS Cushing, a destroyer. The ship was sunk and we all feared that he had been killed. Thanks to God, he wasn't – didn't even get a scratch. He said later that he and several of his ship mater threw a life raft overboard and jumped overboard and managed to make it far enough away from the sinking ship to avoid being sucked under or get burned by the floating and burning fuel. They were able to paddle to an island (Guadalcanal) that was under siege by U.S. Forces, principally Marines, and were able to join them and fight the Japs until the island was captured by the U.S.

Throughout his tour of duty, Calvin sent money home for deposit into a savings account. When he was discharged and returned home, he had enough money to buy the farm where Pa and Ma Thomas lived plus additional adjoining acreage and new farm equipment, including a Farmall Model C Tractor and a used Chevrolet flat bed truck. (I thought that Pa Thomas owned the farm – he didn't, just rented it) by then, both Pa and Ma Thomas were in poor health and moved to Dawson where other children provided for them. Calvin batched it for 3 or 4 years until he married Ruth – who lived down the road about a mile.

It was one of these summers (probably '47) while Calvin was batching that I spent most of the summer with him. He taught me how to drive both the tractor and truck and let me help with the work. I remember once when I was driving the truck the brakes failed and I just aimed it at a small tree and ran it into the tree to stop. It bent the bumper slightly but his only comment was "Quick thinking Bill".

On rainy days we would squirrel hunt or go fishing (just as we had done when I visited Pa Thomas). At night, we often went coon hunting, using his black and tan hound named Bugle Ann. When Bugle Ann got on the trail of a coon and started her mournful cry we often stopped and built a fire and sat and listened to her.

On many nights at the house – we would sit out on the front porch after supper and smoke and talk. I always tried to get him to tell me about the war but he didn't much want to talk about it. Sometimes he would come out with a little tidbit – a couple of which I still remember.

He said that when he joined up with the Marines to chase the Japs off Guadalcanal he took a Springfield rifle and a pistol off a fallen comrade and went hunting for Japs – as if they were squirrels. He came across this grass hut on stilts in the jungle and as he was slipping around the hut a monkey jumped out of the hut and landed on his back – and he messed in his pants. He was sure a Jap had him. He shot the monkey and returned to camp – and never told anyone what happened.

His next assignment was manning a picket boat. His job was to report any Japanese ships or airplanes that he saw or heard – there were two other sailors on the boat but he was the skipper. He said one night they were anchored about a mile out from an island and had finished supper and were sitting out on the deck, smoking and visiting. It got dark and suddenly one of the sailors pointed and asked "What is that thing out there in the water?" It was too dark to say for sure but the other shouted "Darn – it's a mine!" They all jumped into the ocean and swam to shore. The next day another boat took them back to the picket boat – and it was still where they had left it – along with an empty oil drum that was bumping along the side.

One night I asked him "Calvin, how did you manage to save so much money - I didn't think soldier and sailors were paid very much." Calvin answered "You are right – if I saved all of my Seaman's pay, I couldn't have afforded 10 acres and a mule." "But if you promise not to tell a soul – I'll tell you how I got so much money" said Calvin. "I promise" I said. He told me he won it playing poker and shooting craps and in betting on himself. He said "out in the south pacific money didn't mean much - there was nowhere to spend it. So everybody gambled – a lot – and most were not very good at it. He shied away from the good ones. "Tell me about betting on yourself" I said.

He said that a bunk mate of his on the USS Cushing had been a professional prize fighter in Philadelphia. He said no one would spar with him – he was a heavy weight but he finally talked me into getting into the ring with him. Calvin was about 6'3" and 240-250 pounds. (matter of fact, my dad and all of his brothers were about that size). Calvin said the first few times in the ring, his friend whacked him purty good – particularly in the nose which he bloodied. On about the third time in the ring, his friend jabbed him in the nose, made him mad, and he threw a roundhouse right that knocked his friend out. When he came to – he asked if I wanted to learn to box and I said "sure". He started to give me boxing lessons and I soon got purty good at it – I was already very strong and my punch was like a mule kick.

For recreation – we always had boxing matches. I entered a bunch of them and always bet all the money I could scrape up – on myself. I rarely lost and it got hard to find anyone to bet against me. So, I would go to another ship or island where they didn't know me and enter their prize fights – bet and win.

Oh, and another thing I would do was search for dead Japs and take guns, knives, or whatever else I could find off them and sell it to the new replacement that were always coming along.

I made the mistake of telling Calvin that I wanted to go out west and become a cowboy. One day after milking he grabbed me and put me on a cow and swatted her.

She bucked a little then ran under a tree and a limb knocked me off. He thought that was funny. He still had a pair of mules (Spark Plug and Sport) which he used for cultivating mostly. On another occasion, he put a cuckle barn on Spark Plug's back, threw a piece of quilt over it, and lifted me up on top of him, slapped him on the rump and shouted "Start bucking". And Spark Plug responded – with me holding on his mane for dear life. I lasted about 3 bucks then hit the dirt. Calvin said "You ain't going to be no cowboy?

Calvin was a very successful farmer and earned a good living for his family (2 sons and 1 daughter) from his "Navy" farm. He raised tobacco (burly and dark – hickory fired) and beef cattle (Hereford's). Uncle Calvin was one of my heroes – and remained so until he passed away.

CHAPTER 9

VISITS TO OTHER KIN FOLKS

*Uncle Stallard and Aunt Alberta

They lived on a farm a couple of miles from Pa Thomas and didn't have any children. They really spoiled me and I loved it. Uncle Stallard always kept a gentle mare for me to ride – and he had a saddle which was adjusted to fit me. He let me drive the team and help him with whatever he was doing. Aunt Alberta always baked a chocolate cake (my favorite) for me. And we always made a freezer of ice cream.

*Aunt Jessie

Aunt Jessie was a widow who raised two children alone, Arvil and Ermiel. She worked as a "practical" nurse and made extra money sewing – and making quilts. Aunt Jessie was dad's oldest sister. She was very petite and very frugal – they said she pinched her pennies so hard that honest Abe grunted. Like all my relatives, she was an excellent cook and always had a garden – in those days, everyone had a garden. She also grew many flowers and there was always a vase of fresh flowers in her small house. She was a vegetarian I think. I don't ever remember her serving meat. But she made the best vegetable dishes – unique in those days. Many of her dishes were of mixed vegetables – for example, corn, squash, and potatoes; fresh corn and tomatoes (my favorite), macaroni and tomatoes, and the best of all – potato sandwiches.

A potato sandwich was made by slicing the potato very thin (similar to a potato chip - but slightly thicker) and frying them with chopped onions in a covered skillet, add mayonnaise to a couple of slices of bread along with sliced tomatoes – Yummy! Try it sometimes. Another thing I remember is peanut butter mixed with honey and spread on gram crackers.

Aunt Jessie liked to play Chinese checkers and we played many a game. She was a fine Christian lady. Many in the family felt sorry for her – being a widow and all – and were amazed at the amount of money in her estate when she passed away.

I still remember her favorite expression "Well, I declare." Two things stand out in my mind about visits to Aunt Jessie:

(1) First is the "Salty Dog".

Aunt Jessie, to save money, rented a small house in the bad part of town. It was near the edge of town and down the hill from her on Highway 62 was a notorious "Road House" called the The <u>Salty Dog</u>. Dawson historically vacillated between "wet" and "dry" - either way, there was never a shortage of joy juice.

On Saturday nights in the summer I would sit on Aunt Jessie's front porch and listen to all the interesting noises floating up the hill from the Salty Dog. There would be music from the juke box, laughter, cursing, screaming, engines racing, motorcycle noises, an occasional gunshot, glass breaking, and always the siren of the Dawson Police car as it arrived to break up a fight or something. Those coal miners worked hard but on payday - they played even harder.

(2) Trip to the Coal Mine

Uncle-Cousin Arvil went to work at the Dawson Collieries (a shaft mine) right out of high school. One time when I was visiting he forgot his lunch pail. Aunt Jessie was in a tizzie - pore little Arvil (son) was going to be working all day without anything to eat. I finally convinced her to let me take his lunch pail to him. The coal mine was right on Highway 62 - just 2 or 3 miles away. She finally gave in and I picked up the lunch pail and took off for the coal mine.

CHAPTER 10

DOWN INTO THE BOWELS OF THE EARTH

I walked down Alexander Street to Highway 62 and turned left (in front of the Salty Dog, and started walking east on 62 - in about 30 minutes I saw the mine tipple off to my left. Soon I came to the road to the mine and took it. The closer I got to the mine, the noisier it got - rail cars thumping together, coal falling into rail cars, grinding from the shops, engines running and cable winding - and men covered in coal dust moving about. I looked for a familiar face but couldn't tell much - their faces looked like reverse coon faces - black all over with white eyes.

I finally stopped a man (Mr. Taylor) and asked "Where's Arvil? He asked "You mean Arvil Cansler or

Arvil Beshears?" I said "Beshears." He said "He's working down in the mine." I asked "How do I get down in the mine?" He said "Little boys can't go into the mine - it's too dangerous." About that time Woody (who later married Arvil's sister) walked up and asked "Billy, what are you doing out here - is something the matter?" Sanford Taylor said "He wants to go down in the mine to see Arvil Beshears." Woody asked "Does your Mother know you are out here?" I replied "No sir - I spent the night with Aunt Jessie and she sent me out here to bring Arvil's lunch pail."

Woody looked at Sanford and asked "Is it all right with you if I take him down in the mine?" Sanford, who was the boss said, "If you accept responsibility and keep him close to you - go ahead." I was excited as I followed Woody to the mine opening. He stopped by the cable operator and talked to him. We walked over by the rails and waited. He said "You are going to get filthy." I said "Ok". Soon a mine car came down the tracks and stopped. Woody climbed in and reached over and lifted me in. He moved to the end of the car and kicked the cable - and we started moving towards the bowels of the earth. The tunnel had overhead electric lights (about 100 yards apart) and it was silent (except for the noise made by the rail car) and cool. The outside temperature was probably 90 degrees and muggy! Down in the mine it felt like about 70%. (Arvil told me it stayed that temperature - year round).

After what seemed like an hour of traveling down a long, long, hill we started slowing down. We saw a man up ahead and he tripped a switch so that the rail car turned and headed into a side tunnel. After a short ride we came upon a group of men digging coal at the end of this tunnel. The car stopped and we climbed out. The men started loading coal in the car. The man on the big machine (called a joy loader) waved at us. It was Arvil. Soon the car was loaded and started moving back up hill. Arvil got off the machine and walked over to us. He asked Woody "Are you putting sweet William to work?"Woody said naw "Jessie sent him out here with your lunch." I handed Arvil his lunch pail and he thanked me. Woody winked at Arvil and asked me "Billy, how do you plan to get back out of here." I said "walk I guess." They both laughed.

Woody and I soon walked back to the main tunnel where the switch man was. We waited and watched as another empty car passed and went down another side tunnel - returning later - loaded with coal. We waited for what seemed an hour and another car rolled to a stop - except it was a man car complete with benches. We climbed aboard and in awhile were back to the mouth of the tunnel - and got out. I thanked Woody for all his help. He said "Whatever you do - don't ever go to work in the mines" and I didn't.

As I started to walk back to Dawson, a car stopped and gave me a ride. It was Mr. Voorhes - one of the mine owners. Riding back, I asked him "Which miners made the most money?" He smiled and said "The owners - then the professional employees - engineers and geologist." I always remembered that answer.

CHAPTER 11

HELP WANTED – OR VICE VERSA

One thing I learned very early in life was – if you really wanted something – you could obtain it – providing you were willing to work for it. The following are jobs I took and things I did in order to make money.

<u>Mowing Lawns</u>

The first money I earned was from mowing lawns (we called them yards). This really was not a "job" – I immediately became an entrepreneur. The first lawn I remember mowing was our next door neighbor – Mrs. Black. I used her push mower and she paid me 50¢.

I noticed a broken mower in her garage and offered to buy it. She gave it to me and I took the mower to Hopgood's Garage and they welded the piece that was broken. Then I sharpened the blade, oiled it good, and got paint at the 5 and dime store and painted it red., white, and blue – now I was in business. I borrowed dad's clippers and hoe for the first few jobs then bought my own at O'Brien's hardware. The charge for mowing and lawn maintenance ranged from 25¢ to $1. For cutting grass only on a small yard - 25¢. For cutting grass, edging, trimming hedges and shrubs, and hoeing around flowers, etc. - $1. (the latter usually took all day – the former about 2 hours.) I earned about $5 a week – big money in those days.

I hope you noticed that I said push mower. There were no power mowers in those days.

One of the lawns I remember in particular was for Mr. Denny Clark. He had been a local business man (department store) but was retired and semi invalid. He lived in a large house with a very large yard and lots of shrubs. It took all day to do that job but he paid well – a whole dollar. He was heavy into politics and was the democratic party "whip". After I learned to drive I chauffeured him some and got an education in politics. I once drove him to Paducah to meet with Vice President Alben Barkley. Mr. Barkley's advice to me was "Stay out of politics – it's a very nasty business" and I followed his advice.

A couple of things I learned about lawn maintenance were. You always should mow clockwise - - all lawn mowers are designed to throw the cut grass to the right. Therefore, you cut it again and it blends back into compose and improves the soil. Next, do a complete job - mow, edge, trim, weed, hoe flower beds - even though you only contracted to cut the grass. When most folk saw how nice these yards looked when you finished – they nearly always gave you a nice tip - and referred you to others. (another lesson I never forgot).

Carpenter and Woodworker

I was hired by one of the elders at Church (Mr. Hancock) to be his helper in his woodworking shop. He made custom made furniture – tables, chairs, chests, bookcases, cabinets – you name it, he could build it. His shop was equipped with all the tools you could imagine – saws, lathes, drills, sanders, etc. I messed up a lot of lumber but eventually became reasonably proficient in furniture making and finishing – stain, varnish, paint, hand rub , etc. Best I recall, I earned 20¢ an hour.

Most everything was in short supply during the war years and the repair business thrived. One Saturday mom sent me to downtown to get something or another, (I think it was some cloth) and I passed Brantley's Shoe Repair. Both my shoes had holes worn in the soles and I put cardboard in them to cover the holes (a common practice in those days). Anyway, on an impulse I went into the "shoe shop" and inquired how much it would cost to fix my shoes. Mr. Brantley told me 50¢ for half soles only and $1 for half soles and new heels.

I reached in my pocket and checked my funds – a dollar bill and 4 dimes. The dollar was what mom had given me to purchase whatever it was I came to town for – the 40¢ was mine. When I turned around I saw a hand written sign in the glass merchandise case which Mr. Brantley was standing behind - it said <u>Help Wanted</u>. I told him I only had 40¢ and he said "That's O.K. – you can pay me later." (He was a good friend and lodge brother of my dad). Mr. Gaines, the "shine boy" spoke up and said "No – I'll pay for the boy". (Byron Gaines was the only Negro in Dawson in those days – I had met him before at a baseball game and we had talked about the Saint Louis Cardinals – the favorite team of both).

I finally said to Mr. Brantley "I've got a better idea – if you will give me a job you can deduct it from my wages." To my amazement, he said "You've got a deal". I looked at Byron who was smiling broadly and I asked "when do I start." Mr. Brantley said "Now – my helper was drafted into the army last week and I'm really behind.

I told him I had to get something at Hayes Dry Goods and take it to my Mother but would be right back. I rushed out of the shoe shop, made my purchase, and took it home and told her about my new job. She asked

"What about the job you already have with Mr. Hancock?"

Then it hit me . I hadn't even thought about that. I finally said "I'll go by and tell him." She proceeded to lecture me around always "doing the right thing, etc.") She was right of course – I should have given Mr. Hancock at least two week's notice (according to mom) before I quit so he could find a replacement. I left and on the way to Hancock's wood working shop I kept thinking of a solution to the problem I had created for myself. (The reason I wasn't working for Mr. Hancock that Saturday was because he told me not to come – he had something else to do.)

Before I got to Hancock's shop I heard the saw buzzing and when I went inside Mr. Hancock looked up with a very surprised look on his face. The other person in the shop operating the saw was a grown man. Mr. Hancock led me outside and said, "I thought I told you not to come to work today." I said "I didn't come to work – I came to talk to you about something." He asked "What"? I said "My job)".

To my amazement, he bowed his head and looked guilty as he said "I wasn't going to tell you until next weekend – and then I was going to help you find another job." He explained that the man inside the shop was the new Preacher for our Church. He was also an experienced and skilled cabinet maker and needed an extra job to support his large family. I said "That's ok – I understand." He beamed and said "Let's go inside and I'll introduce you." We went inside and I met the Reverend Diech – our new Pastor and the solution to my problems. I turned to leave and Mr. Hancock asked "was that what you came to talk about?" I said "No sir, I came to tell you I had a new job." He said "The Lord sometimes works in strange ways" and I responded "I know". I skipped my way to the shoe shop whistling "High Ho" (a song from the movie <u>Snow White</u>).

Shoe Cobbler

When I arrived at the shoe shop there were 3 or 4 customers inside – complaining because their shoes weren't ready. Mr. Brantley was working as fast as he could to repair their shoes. I watched, as soon as he repaired a pair, he gave them to Byron who polished them and wrapped them in brown paper. The next pair repaired, I helped Byron polish. Soon, everyone was taken care of and Mr. Brantley said "Take off your shoes." I did and he gave me my first lesson in shoe repair. First, you pulled off the heel with a claw hammer, next you cut off the sole just where it started at the heel, then you selected a pair of replacements half soles (leather or composition (rubber) and glued them on, then stitched them around the edge, then nailed them on the end by the heel, then nailed on the heel, the – trimmed them and ground them smooth around the edge, then applied solid shoe wax and polished the edge on a rotating brush, then gave them to Byron to polish the uppers. (Not all shoe repair shops polished the uppers – this was just an "extra service" that Brantley's provided).

I spent the balance of that first Saturday, working mostly on rough miners steel toed boots and farmers rough lace up boots. The stitching was the hardest task to master but eventually I became proficient in shoe repair and shoe polishing. Plus I learned a great deal about sports, listing to Byron talk to his sit down customers.

The shoe shop was a gathering place for the local sports fans. There was always a "game" on the radio – either St. Louis Cardinals or Cincinnati Reds baseball, Murry State, Western Kentucky, or University of Kentucky basketball, or Notre Dame, U.K, or Tennessee football.

We worked until near 8 p.m. that first Saturday – I made two trips to the "Squeeze In" café for hamburgers and RC colas. Before I went home in my "new" shoes, Mr. Brantley gave me three dollar bills. I calculated in m head ($2.00 ÷ 8 hours = 37 ½ ¢ per hour) that was 87.5% more than my former job – and much more exciting!

For reasons unknown to me, the shoe shop went out of business and the owner moved to Michigan. I was unemployed for awhile.

Paper Route

I got a bicycle for Christmas around the fifth or sixth grade – don't remember exactly. Anyway, it was a beauty – a Hawthorne from Montgomery Wards. (In those days, you ordered many things from the "wish book" – a catalog from either Spiegel's, Sears Roebuck, or Montgomery Ward's – all out of Chicago I think). I soon became a very "expert" bike rider and won my share of bike races.

One day I was reading the "want ads" in the Dawson Progress and saw this ad "paper route for sale". By then we had a telephone and I called the number. It was Rupert Bert and he wanted to sell his Courier Journal paper route. I told him I was very interested so we arranged to meet at Woodburn's Pharmacy to discuss it. We met and he showed me a crude map with his route plotted out on it and a list of his customers, etc. He was asking $50.00 for it. I argued that was too much. However, after he explained that the $50 included a $25 bond at the courier Journal in Louisville which he would transfer to me and that his profit was between $8 to $10 per week – I reconsidered. However, I asked to help him a couple of mornings before I made a decision. He agreed.

I stopped at the Western Auto Store and had a big heavy duty basket installed on my bicycle. The next morning I met Rupert at the Depot at 4:30 a.m. Shortly after I arrived the Illinois Central Train from Louisville pulled in at the station and a large bundle of newspapers was unloaded onto a baggage cart. Rupert pulled the cart oven to a spot next to the station, cut the grass rope holding the bundle together, and started rolling papers and putting a heavy rubber band around each. Later he stuffed them into two canvass paper bags – he took one and I the other. We started the "route". By 6:00 a.m. we were finished.

We repeated this process the next day and at the conclusion we went to the "Squeeze In" and got some hot chocolate and donuts and did the paper work and I paid the $50 (from my savings of roughly $100). Now I was an entrepreneur. I kept the route for a couple of years and sold it for $100.

The most difficult things about throwing a paper route are (1) weather (2) dogs, and (3) collecting. After a year you really appreciate the postman, the milk deliveryman, and everyone who works outside in all sorts of weather, particularly those that must meet a schedule every day. The most miserable mornings of my life were delivering newspapers in a deep snow. It was impossible to ride the bike so I had to sling the bag over my shoulder and walk – it took several trips back to the depot before I would finish.

Then, there were always 3 or 4 dogs in town that would bite – some would try to tear a leg off. I tried rocks, bb gun, baseball bat, etc. before I finally came up with a solution. I cut a piece of well rope in a length of about 3 feet. Then I folded it double and wrapped it with about 3 layers of bailing wire – leaving a loop that I could get my hand through. Next, I covered the wire with a layer of friction tape. I kept this weapon in my paper bag and over time knocked every dog that tried to bite me unconscious. Soon, they tucked tail and ran and hid when they saw me coming. I lost a couple of customers who claimed I was trying to kill their pets.

Collecting was a valuable experience. I soon learned you could classify your customers into two categories. (A) Those that intended to pay but didn't have the money, and (B) those that had the money but did not intend to pay. The latter were the worse. Except during school, vacation, the only time I had to collect was the weekend. Every Saturday after I made deliveries I went home for breakfast, ate, then we back over my route collecting.

I had a customer receivable book and kept a careful record of collections. After I made the round, I went by the post office and bought a money order and sent it to the Courier Journal to pay for my papers. Whatever money I had left was my "profit" – also, whatever I had not collected was also my "profit" – <u>unrealized</u>.

A couple of memorable collection efforts were:

I knocked on the door of a young divorcee who lived in an apartment building. She came to the door in a robe and barefoot. I explained my purpose. She stood there a minute, then said as she loosened her belt" I don't have any money today but I have something better than money that you might like (as her robe came opened and I stood there gaping – looking at her boobs and privates). I backed off and handed her an addressed envelope and said "Just send me the money when you get it – and scampered away.

There was a railroad engineer that lived at the top of Meadows Hill. I could never catch him at home and he owed me for about 2 months – about $6. I finally caught him at home one Saturday morning. Matter of fact, I woke him up by pounding on his door. He came to the door in his long johns – wiping the sleep out of his eyes. He was a huge man – over 6 feet and about 250 pounds. He looked at me and demanded in a gruff voice "What the heck do you want?" I stood my ground and replied "I want my darn money – you owe me $6 for the newspaper." He said "I ain't here to read the paper – I don't owe you nothing." I said "you never cancelled and I brought your paper every day – so pay up." He said "What in heck are you going to do if I don't pay."

I stood straight and looked up into his eyes and said "I'm going to go get my dog Charmer out of my paper bag and beat heck out of you." He started to laugh, went back into the bedroom and returned with a $10 bill and handed it to me and said "Keep the change Spunky – I don't feel like getting whipped this morning."

Picking Peaches

One summer, Tom Hopkins and I answered a newspaper ad for farm help. We ended up spending the summer with a farm family near Paducah that had a huge commercial orchard – peaches and apples. Fred, the owner, had been in a car wreck and couldn't work – so Marge, his wife, placed the add. Under her direction, Tom and I literally harvested the crop for them. No big deal – so why mention this. There were two episodes from this adventure I'll tell you about.

The first involved "quitting smoking." Tom and I both smoked cigarettes – Lucky strikes (without filters). I started when I was 14 – and still do. We ran out of cigarettes during the week and it was about 5 miles to the nearest store. Tom suggested we just quit. I didn't want to until he made this proposition – "The first to smoke a cigarette would give his next pay check to the other. (We were paid twice a month - $100 each. I agreed. We went for several days without nicotine – chewing on limbs – eating peaches – sucking on peach seeds, etc. and growing more irritable by the day.

Then the day came when we were picking peaches in the same tree. His ladder on one side of the tree – mine on the other. We both reached for the same peach and were eyeball to eyeball – and read each (without saying a word), others mind. We climbed down the ladder, got on the tractor, and headed for the country store and each brought a carton of Lucky Strikes. We chain smoked all the way back to the orchard and took numerous "smoke" break the rest of the day.

The other occurred one night at the dinner table. We slept in the fruit shed but ate with Fred, Margie and their two young sons. Margie got up from the table and took

Fred's glass to refill it with iced tea. She accidentally dropped the glass and it shattered. I said "You dropped your glass eye Marge" and Tom and I just hooted. Everyone else was silent. Marge returned to the table, sat down, and gave me a mean look. Fred, who was in a wheel chair, said "Bill, I know you were just trying to be funny – but – Marge really does have a glass eye."

I never learned and still stick my foot in my mouth on occasion.

Grocery Store Clerk

When I was about 15 I got a job at Cluck's Grocery where my mom got her groceries. Cluck's was a typical pre-supermarket small town grocery store. Most staples were in the <u>bulk</u> and meat was not packaged – each store had a butcher and butcher shop. Groceries were sold on credit and most were delivered. Many customers called in their orders. Therefore, it required several "clerks" to operate the store. Saturday was, by far, the business day and the store was closed on Sunday. The key people were Mr. Cluck – owner, Virginia – bookkeeper, Harry - Butcher, and Juanita – chief clerk. I worked on Saturdays only and started as a clerk. We had sales pads and you had to write down everything – customers name and address, item description, price, quantity, and total. Most of the time I waited on customers in person –but occasionally (if Juanita and Virginia were busy), I would take a call in order.

The biggest problem was the price. Most canned and packaged items had a paper price label glued on them but the glue would fail and labels fall off. There were no prices anywhere on produce or bulk items (flour, sugar, beans, lard, etc.). Harry's writing was bad and you had to interpret the meat prices. All dry long you would hear clerks yelling "How much is sugar?" "How much are potatoes?" It was a madhouse sometimes.

Most of the customers were farmers and coal miners. Almost all the coal miners purchased their groceries on credit as did some of the farmers. And many farmers did some barter. Then would trade eggs, butter, produce, etc. for groceries. Mr. Cluck would handle most of the barter transactions. He would hand you a piece of paper with an amount written on it and say "give them credit for this" and Virginia watched the credit sales." She might approach the customer and say "Mrs. Jones, your balance has gotten too high – we can't sell you any more on credit unless you pay your account down some" the customer might open her purse and pull out a $20 bill and hand it to her". Then Virginia might say to me "Let her have $10 worth on credit." It really got bad if the coal mines shut down, or if the miners went on strike, or if there was a tobacco crop failure. I was poor too and really sympathize with these poor people. This was a good early lesson in "raw economics."

To earn extra money I would make deliveries Saturday night after the store closed. (I knew how to drive but didn't have a license). Cluck had a battered old Ford pickup truck and he or Harry would stay late and help me load up – usually 100 pound sacks of sugar and/or grain plus groceries. They would had me an empty paper sack with a crude map. (The destination was always on a dirt roadway out in the country). On it and might say – "someone will meet you at the barn and help you unload. They will pay you in cash for the ticket - $45.00. Here's $15.00 for change." This was my introduction to another business in the local economy – "moonshine." (The grain and sugar were used to make moonshine whiskey.)

I worked at Cluck's until I graduated from high school and went to Michigan.

CHAPTER 12

THE FOUR MUSKETEERS

I think the "Four Musketeers" teamed up in about the sixth grade – myself, Rodney ("Rod") Lamb, Doug "Cody Hamby" and John Bradley "Buddy" Hazel. We were like brothers and inseparable through high school – then went our separate ways. Rodney to the Marine Corps, then a degree in engineering from U.K. and a career in the concrete pipe business; Doug attended U.K. and dropped out, got married, and bought a radio station in Providence; Buddy moved to Michigan and went into the ice cream business – and died at an early age.

We all loved the great outdoors - camping, hunting, and fishing. We were in the Boy Scouts together and Rodney and I (both Eagle Scouts) went to the first

Canadian Scout Jamboree. We were sponsored by the Dawson Lions Club (they paid our expenses) and when we returned we put on a program at about every Lions Club in West Kentucky. I have fond memories of our scout master – Lamar Merck. (see next chapter).

At about 8th grade, Rodney and I also built a boat and used it all summer on Piney Creek.(Separate book about this adventure "A Summer on Piney Creek").

I remember Brady McClain very well. He was the local game warden and the sponsor for the Junior Conservation club. All four of us joined the club and Brady decided to enter a 4 man rifle team in the Kentucky marksman tournament. Need I say who the 4 team members were – us, of course. We won the state championship in 1945 – thanks to Brady and government ammunition. Somehow, Brady came up with .22 ammo (which was scarce as hen's teeth in those days) and we got a lot of good training and practice. I was helped also by the gift of a German .22 cal. Mauser rifle which my Uncle Herman brought back from the war and gave to me. It was an extremely accurate .22 rifle.

We all loved to hunt squirrels and Brady would sometimes take us to a real good hunting area (usually near one of the game preserves he patrolled) and leave us to hunt while he made his rounds. Naturally, he also provided the "practice" ammo for our hunts. We loved that man.

Of the four of us, I suppose I was the most devout hunter – and fisherman too, for that matter – and continued to love both sports for my entire life.

There was a coon hunter that lived about a mile from us named Dick Long. He was a coal miner and everyone called him "Old Feller". I was highly honored the first time he invited me to go coon hunting with him. (Little did I know that he wanted me along to climb the tree and shake the coons out – which I did). In no time I became a regular on all of Old Feller's coon hunts. (some of our most memorable hunts are in my book ("Hickory Fired Tobacco, Moonshine Whiskey, Beautiful Women, and Fast Horses").

At about that time Dawson hosted the National Coon Hunt. The Old Feller had a young coon hound which he called "Jeff" and he paid the entry fee and entered him into the "coon tracking" contest. I know that was a mistake for Jeff had not been broke from chasing deer and I knew there were deer in the area where they were having the contest.

Sure enough, after the dogs were released on the coon trail (they had drug a coon in a burlap bag - (toe sack) and had gone about 200 yards, a big buck jumped up and Jeff and a couple of other coon hounds took off after him. The next day a farmer from Crabtree called Old Feller and told him he had caught his dog. We went and got him and that was the last of the big coon hunt for us.

Swimming

School wasn't bad during the winter. It was too cold to play outside. But come spring and when it started warming up – school could be mighty confining. We used to sit in the study hall and plan what we were going to do when school let out for the summer.

Dawson had some summer attractions that not many small towns had to offer:

*Tradewater *State Park *Pennyrile Park

All involved water – which provided a place to swim and to fish. All of us became good swimmers at an early age.

The Tradewater river passed on the west side of Dawson. Its headwaters were in Christian county and it emptied into the Ohio River near Olney. Although it was polluted by the coal mines, it was ok to swim in it. Matter of fact, the coppers water would heal wounds (scratches) on your body. There was a rope swing in a big tree on the bank behind Rodney's house and we used to swing out over the river on the rope and drop off into the water. Most of the time we were naked.

Another swimming hole on the river was the old mill dam by Schwab's Used Furniture Store – west of downtown. The river was dammed by a concrete dam and was deep – you could climb a tree on the bank and dive in. In the olden days there had been a grist mill there that ground corn.

It was also fun to boat ride on the Tradewater. We usually had a .22 rifle with us and hunted squirrels as we padded up the river. There weren't many fish though – the pollution killed most everything except a few "rough" fish – gar, carp and buffalo (drum). The creeks feeding into the river had lots of fish though.

The State Park had been built by the W.P.A. during the depression. It was about 3 miles north east of Dawson. It contained a beautiful deep lake surrounded by hills and woods as well as a shelter house, bath house, and picnic tables. There was a nice swimming area with a sandy beach and diving board. The lake was well stocked with fish – bass, perch, and catfish.

We would usually walk to the State Park and spend the entire day swimming and diving. They sold hot dogs and cokes at the bath house. It cost a dime to use the dressing room and shower. It was here that the boys learned that the female anatomy was slightly different from the male. Some of the bathing suits worn by the girls were really tight fitting – except for J.M. – she always wore a two piece suit and now and then the top part (I think they call it a halter) would come loose and expose her boobies. I now believe she did that on purpose. Buddy always claimed that he dived under water once when that happened and felt of them – and she let him or so he said?

We were all excellent swimmers.

The spill way behind the dam on the State Park lake was Papa Bell's favorite fishing holes. When he was staying with us during the summer, he would get a spade and can and go out in our garden and collect a can of worms. Then he would ask me "Bill, I've got some worms – want to go fishing." Of course, my answer was always "Yes". He would tell mom "Edith, if you will fix us a sack lunch, I'll take Bill out to the State Park and we'll catch a mess of fish for supper." Mom nearby always approved – she loved fish. Many times my cousins Jimmy and Bubbie went with us.

We would get the fishing poles, can of worms, and sack lunch and take the short cut route to the lake – walking of course. The short cut was across pasture land and farms. When we arrived at the spill way, Papa Bell would start fishing in the deep holes by the dam. If he started catching fish immediately, I would bait my line and drop it in close to his. He would scold me and make me move. If he wasn't getting bites, I would take a few worms from the can, put them in my pocket, and move down the creek that the spillway fed into and fish at each likely looking hole I came to. If I caught a fish, I would cut a small limb and make a stringer and put the fish on it.

Sometimes I might travel at least a mile down the creek – until I had a stringer full of fish. Then I would rejoin Papa Bell – who usually had a stringer containing more fish than mine. We would eat our lunch and visit for about an hour before resuming fishing. He would tell me tales of his railroading days.

If we were running out of worms, I would start turning over rocks and catching crickets, worms, etc. – there was always something. Late in the afternoon we would walk back home, clean the fish, and mom would fry them to a golden crisp along with fried potatoes, hush puppies, and a big bowl of cole slaw.   Mighty fine eating. The State Park is now a 4H Camp.

The Pennyrile Park was much further from Dawson – about 10 miles south of Dawson. Too far to walk. Unless we got a ride with someone – we didn't make it to the Pennyrile until the motor bike era arrived. The earlier trips were a treat – later they became routine.

The Pennyrile was the result of the Roosevelt reconstruction days following the great depression. In addition to a large beautiful lake, it contained a large lodge (with large dining room), cabins, golf course, swimming area with bath house, beach, and large diving platform. It was, and still is, a real tourist attractions.

The negative factor was – the park could get overrun with soldiers. There was a large army fort outside

Hopkinsville (29 miles south of Dawson). Fort Campbell, home of the 11th Airborne (paratroopers). The Pennyrile Park was one of their favorite hang outs. They came in droves and brought much beer and booze with them. We were jealous of them became they dated (and married) many of the local girls. Many of them had cars and motorcycles – and money.

When we caught any of them on the diving platform we would dare them to dive off the top (about 40 feet from the water). Many would jump – but few would dive. I remember one in particular who was drunk and bragging. I bet him a quarter that he wouldn't dive from the top platform. He said he would if I would – big mistake. We all dove off the top all the time – especially Rod and me.

Rod was with me and we climbed the stairs to the top – brave paratrooper in tow. I dove first followed by Rod. We swam away from the landing zone and yelled challenges at the drunken paratrooper. Finally, after our taunts "chicken" and encouraging yells from his buddies – he dove. As he fell through the air with arms and legs flaring he was letting out a blood curdling scream - then "SPLASH". What a belly whooper – but it sure sobered him up. He swam straight to shore – not stopping to collect his quarter.

After we began courting, the Pennyrile Park was our favorite place to park and smooch. I'll always have fond memories of that place.

Later in life and after I had a family – we would sometimes stay at the lodge so my children could swim and enjoy the Pennyrile Park.

Graveyard Cleaning

Another memorable summer activity (ATBA – After Transportation Became Available) was attending "Graveyard Cleaning". At a country graveyard cleaning, all the local (area around cemetery) men would bring tools and mow the grass, chop weeds, mend fences, straighten headstones, etc. – cleanup the cemetery and make it pretty. The women folks in the meantime would set a huge table and display the food they prepared. There was always enough food to feed 3 or 4 times the number of participants (in the eating contest that followed). Each of the women had their specialties and it almost became a cooking contest.

A typical layout would consist of n numerous platters, bowls, etc. of the following:

Meats	Vegetables	Deserts
Ham – baked, boiled, fried	Potatoes – mashed, boiled, and fried	Pie – you name it cakes –
Chicken - baked, boiled, fried & chicken & dumplings	Green beans Black eyed peas	chocolate, strawberry,
Turkey-roasted	Tomatoes	yellow,
Beef – roast & stew	Potato salad	coconut, etc.
Meatloaf	Beets	Homemade ice
Squirrel – fried and stew	Corn – fried & boiled Dressing	cream, canned peaches, cookies

Plus salads, breads, watermelons, iced tea, RC colas. There were dozens of country cemeteries around Dawson and they always put an announcement of an upcoming graveyard cleaning in the Dawson Progress. When we spotted them, we would hop on our bikes and ride, to the feast.

CHAPTER 13

OUR FIRST CAR – A MODEL A FORD

We were sitting under a shade tree at Menser's grocery, eating moon pies and washing them down with R.C. colas and Buddy said "I don't know about you boys but I'm getting tired of peddling my legs off every time we go somewhere." (Buddy, Rodney and I had bicycled out to Doug's house for a game of basketball – it was probably 5 miles from Dawson) I asked "anybody got any ideas?"

We sipped and though and Rodney finally said "Yup – why don't we buy a car?" Doug said "between the four of us we couldn't scrape up enough money to buy a little red wagon – much less a car. Are you nuts?"

Rod bristled up and nearly got mad but took a big gulp of R.C., cooled off a minute, and finally said. "Here is what I'm thinking – my granddad is shutting down his sawmill near Olney. I heard him tell my dad that he would probably just leave(abandon) the old wore out Model A Ford that has powered the saw blade. If he still intends to do that, I'll ask him to give it to us."

Doug said "that ain't right – let's offer to buy it from him." Rod said "Fine – what are we going to offer? He looked around at each of us.

I was the first to respond – "I've been saving up to buy a pump shotgun and I've got about three dollars saved – that's my starter for the deal." Buddy said "I've got two dollars and I'm sure my dad will lend me another dollar next payday." My grandmother just gave me two dollars and a half for my birthday, and I've collected nearly a case of coke bottles – if you will give me your empties that will fill the case and I can sell them for 48¢. That would make me three dollars also," said Doug.

Rod said "I've saved a little money myself so do we agree to an offer of twelve dollars for the old Model A?" Yeah – yeah – yeah came from around the circle. Rod continued "you know that my granddad said it's wore out." Buddy said "That's ok – my Uncle has a filling station and garage – I think I can get him to fix it for us – just for the cost of parts."

I said, there is an old rusty Model A in that gully behind the depot – we could probably scavenge some parts from it. Rod said "I'll offer granddad twelve dollars and let you all know tomorrow what he says – I'm sure he will take us up or the deal."

We were getting on our bicycles and ready to peddle back to Dawson when Rod yelled "Stop – there is something I failed to mention." Buddy asked "What?"

Rod said "There is a wheel missing - they took it off to replace it with a pulley wheel to drive the belt for the saw. I said, "I'll take one off the old junked one by the depot."

The next day we got together at Woodburn's Drug Store and Rodney said his granddad wouldn't sell the old Model A to us. We sadly look around at on another - very disappointed. Then Rod said "He wouldn't sell it to us - but he would <u>give</u> it to us.

He was going to haul it to Doug's place tomorrow and unload it in the barn. Frowns turned to grins - we were elated. We agreed to meet at Doug's tomorrow and get started on our "project". I went home and got some tools and picked up Buddie and we went by Hopgood's and bought a wheel for the old Model A. We also spotted a shop manual for a Model A Ford and Mr. Hopgood said we could come by - anytime and read it. He also said he carried Model A parts. The next day we met at Doug's and got started. First we replaced the pulley with the wheel. Then we scrapped off some of the grease and mud. The tires were flat so Doug got a bunch of rags and we stuffed them inside the tires - who needed air. There was no gas cap so we used rags for that also. Doug found some Wooden dynamite boxes that we wired to the frame for seats.

It was leaking oil pretty bad so I took a piece of wood and whittled out a new oil plug and drove it in tight. There was some exposed wiring that Rod fixed with friction tape. We found a couple of buckets and Mr. Hamby took Doug to Dawson and got a bucket of gas and a bucket of used cylinder oil.

We put water in the radiator, gas in the tank, and some oil in the crank case.

Then, it was time for a trail. Rodney, who had been instructed by his granddad, became the driver. Doug, Bud, and I became the "starters." We took turns "twisting its tail" (turning the crank which spun the engine.) It "hit" a couple of times and it seemed like we cranked for an hour before it finally started.

We all climbed on and Rod drove it out of the barn to the back pasture. We rode around the pasture for about an hour before driving back to the barn. Wow! That was fun. The buckets were wired to the frame and became a permanent part of Model A.

During the next several weeks and months that old Model A Ford became a hunting vehicle and a training vehicle. We would all climb aboard with our guns and drive slowly through the fields of the Hamby farm and adjoining farms and shoot at whatever we scared up - usually rabbits. We had much more success at night using carbide lamps to spot "eyes."

We each learned to drive - but nearly burned up the clutch in the process. We learned auto mechanics by trial and error, supplemented by studying the shop manual at Hopgood's garage.

The Menser grocery was about a quarter mile east of Hamby's farm on Highway 62. We would get gas there. However, the Model A was not licensed and none of us had a drivers license so we cut across the adjoining farm and went in to the store from the back. We usually got an R.C. cola and moon pie every time we were at Menser's grocery.

There were two different incidents that happened when we bought gas. The first was when Mrs. Capps (owner's wife) came out to put in the 25¢ worth of gas we bought. She was confused as to which hole to pump the gas into. Rod spoke up and said "It don't make any difference - that ole Sinclair gas you sell is half and half (gas/water) anyway. She took off the radiator cap but before she could insert the gas nozzle, Doug hopped out, grabbed the nozzle and said "Here, let me help. I apologize for Rodney - he was just kidding you."

On another occasion, Mr. Capps came out to help and asked "How can I help you boys?" I replied "You can pump in 25¢ worth of gas - if you can get the rag out." He became very upset and said "I'll have you know we have raised six kids, I work at the mines as well as run this store - and no snot nose kid is going to tell me to "Get the rag out."

   There I went again - foot in my mouth.

A WILD SHOT IN THE DARK

PICTURES AND STUFF

Description	Page
Bill R. Thomas - at age 26	146
Otho E. Thomas - my dad	147
Edith Lurlene (Bell) Thomas - my mom	148
Bill, Loretta (sister), Jim and Bub (cousins)	149
Jim, Papa Bell, and me	149
More first cousins	150
Me and Sis	151
Mom, Dad, & Ollie (Mom's best friend)	152
Great grandmother	152
Me in Michigan	152
Rifle Team - Champs	153
Boy Scout - court of Honor	154
Me and Rod - Canadian Scout Jamboree	155
Grandmother Thomas	156
Dad and his siblings	157
Two Accomplishments	158

Bill R. Thomas

at age 26

My Dad

Otho Elehue Thomas

My Mom

Edith Lurlene Thomas

Bill R. Thomas, Loretta Bell Thomas, (sister) Glenn (Bubbie) and James Boyd Bell (cousins)

James Boyd Bell, Lynn Boyd Bell and Bill R. Thomas

ARNOLD THOMAS
Receives B. S. Degree Tonight

JAMES BOYD BELL
Receives B. S. Degree May 24

BILLY R. THOMAS
Receives B. S. Degree Tonight

Three Local Boys Receive B. S. Degrees

Three local boys, all graduates of Dawson Springs High School, received or will receive degrees from colleges during commencement exercises this spring.

They are Arnold Thomas, 26, son of Mr. and Mrs. Forest Thomas; James Boyd Bell, 22, son of Mr. and Mrs. Fratis Bell, and Billy R. Thomas, 22, son of Mr. and Mrs. Otho E. Thomas.

Arnold Thomas will receive a B. S. degree in Pharmacy from University of Kansas City, School of Pharmacy, tonight. He graduated from high school here in 1946. He is now employed at the Woodburn Rexall Drugs.

James Boyd Bell graduated from the Bowling Green Business University on May 24 with a B. S. degree in Higher Accounting. He was a member of the 1950 graduating class of the local high school.

Billy R. Thomas will receive his B. S. degree in Accounting this evening at the University of Kentucky, Lexington. He will also be commissioned a second lieutenant in the United States Air Force Reserve. He graduated from Dawson Springs High School in 1950.

First Cousins

Bill R. Thomas and sister, Loretta Bell Thomas

Edith Bell, Otho Thomas & Ollie Carmon

Bill's Great Grandmother,
Pernecia Calvina Downs

Bill in Flint, Michigan

Jr. Conservation Club Wins State Rifle Meet at Frankfort

Pictured above are the boys belonging to the Junior Conservation Club who recently won trophies in the state rifle and moskeet meet, held in Frankfort. Upper photo, left to right—Douglas Hamby, Paulus Maass, Bill Thomas, Rodney Lamb, J. B. McClain, and Buddy Hazel. Lower photo, front row, left to right—Dickie Holeman, William Ray Johnson, Norris Turner, Donnie Hazel. Back row, left to right—Jackie Oglesby, Paulus Maass, J. B. McClain, and Donnie Inglis.

Three Dawson Springs Boy Scouts took top honors at the semi-annual Court of Honor of the Hopkins-Webster District held in Madisonville last Thursday, June 16. Rev. J. Edward Cayce, right, presented Buddy Hazel, second from right, with the Eagle Scout Badge. Carroll Morrow, left, presented Billy Ray Thomas, second from left, and Rodney Lamb, center, with Gold Eagle Scout Palms. The three Scouts are members of Troop 14, Dawson Springs.

Boy Scouts' Court Of Honor, Honors Local Scout Troop 14

Two Local Scouts Attending Camp In Ottawa, Canada

Billy Ray Thomas, son of Mr. and Mrs. Otho Thomas, and Rodney Lamb, son of Mrs. Tina Lamb, left for Toledo, O., Monday, where they will join a group of Boy Scouts from other states to attend the Canadian Jamboree at Ottawa, Canada. Thomas and Lamb are both Eagle Scouts and members of the local Troop 14. They will Dawson Springs about

Troop 14 Members Elect New Officers

Members of Troop 14, Boy Scouts, elected Bill Thomas junior assistant Scoutmaster, and Bill Ford senior patrol leader at Monday night's meeting of the local troop.

2nd Lt. Bill R. Thomas Called To Active Duty In U. S. Air Force

2nd Lt. Bill R. Thomas, son of Mr. and Mrs. Otho Thomas, city, has been called to active duty in the U. S. Air Force.

He will report to Lackland Air Force Base, San Antonio, Texas,

Two Eagle Scouts To Give Rotary Program

Eagle Scouts Billy Ray Thomas and Rodney Lamb will supply the Rotary Club program for Monday night's meeting. The two scouts, both members of the local Troop 14, will give their report on the Canadian Jamboree they attended recently.

Billy Ray Thomas, son of Mr. and Mrs. Otho E. Thomas, was initiated into the Alpha Mu Chapter of the Beta Alpha Psi fraternity December 8, 1952. Beta Alpha Psi is a national accounting honorary fraternity. The Alpha Mu Chapter is located on the campus of University of Kentucky at Lexington.

Billy R. Thomas Leaves For Accountant Training

Billy R. Thomas, son of Mr. and Mrs. Otho E. Thomas, left this morning for New York City where he will attend a six-weeks training program of Haskins and Sells, Certified Public Accountants.

Thomas graduated this year from the University of Kentucky, Lexington, with a degree in Accounting.

Upon completion of the training program Thomas will go to Cincinnati, Ohio, where he will be employed in the firm's office there.

Remember When? . . . .

THIS GROUP posed for the photographer in 1902 at the Alexander Place in Caldwell County.

Bill's grandmother, Matilda Jane Mitchell (center - on right side of boy in the hat.)

Macedonia School - Christian County, Kentucky - appx. 1918

Otho E. Thomas - Top row, second from right
Cora Thomas   - 2nd row from top - third from left
Stallard Thomas - 3rd row from top, second from left
Lucretia Thomas - Bottom row, third from left

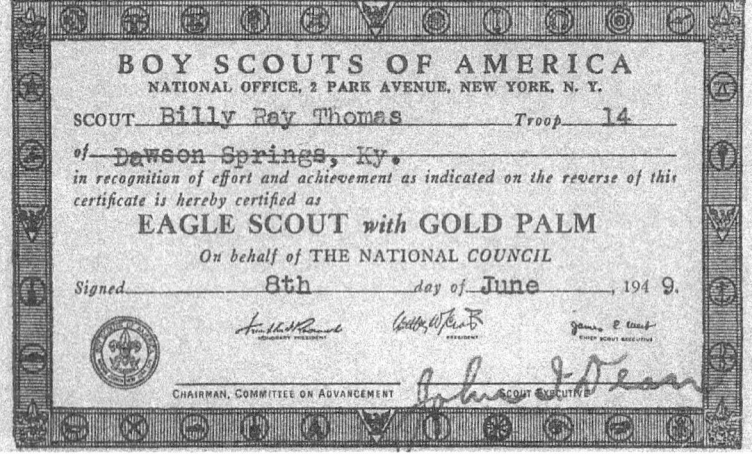

CHAPTER 14

BE PREPARED

There was an active Boy Scout Troop (Troop 14) that met in my Church (First Christian). The scout master was Mr. Merck. His son, Lamar, was Jr. Assistant Scout Master. My mom, encouraged me to join the boy scouts and as soon as I was eligible (age 12), so I did. I decided very early on that I wanted to become an Eagle Scout – and conveyed that desire to Mr. Merck. He and Lamar helped me along as I methodically advanced though the ranks. Tenderent, second class, first, class, star, life, then finally, Eagle.

I went to summer camp one summer at Camp Hogg, in Owensporo. (Since closed) While there, I was inducted into the "Order of the Arrow."

I continued in scouting until high school and obtained the Gold cluster for my Eagle Scout Badge. As best I recall I finally accumulated 52 Merit Badges.

Rod and I went to the first Canadian boy scout jamboree in Ottaura, Ontario (next chapter).

P.S.

As an adult I served as Assistant Scout Master in Dallas and both my sons attained the rank of Eagle Scout. So did many of their friends. I am very proud of them.

CHAPTER 15

THE FIRST CANADIAN BOY SCOUT JAMBOREE

I never knew the reason but will forever be thankful and indebted to the Dawson Springs Lions Club for sponsoring both Rod and me for our trip to the very first Canadian Boy Scot Jamboree in Ottawa, Canada in 1949 (I always thought Scoutmaster Merck had a lot to do with it).

Anyway, the Lions Club provided a round trip bus ticket to Ottawa and as I recall, plus $10 each for meals. This was our first trip out of the states and most memorable trip up to then.

When we arrived at the camp grounds we were in awe. There were hundreds of tents and boy scouts from everywhere - more than 2,500 of them (more than the population of Dawson). We got situated and started exploring and meeting other scouts. We had been advised before we left to take plenty of "trade goods". Trading was going on everywhere we went. We took a bunch of troop 14 neckerchiefs and got right into trading early. I came home with all sorts of good stuff I traded for - badges. , neckerchiefs, etc. We met the oldest US Scout - Uncle Otto (I think he was a Mr. Otto C. Horoung - not sure).

The area covered was so large that it was impossible to see everything. There were exhibits of everything imaginable in scouting. But the most interesting thing was to visit with scouts from all over the world.

There always were visitors wandering throughout the camp - mostly Canadians. I met a French Canadian girl name of Pierette Le Blanc that I corresponded with for a year or longer after I returned home. She was very beautiful and intelligent. (I always wondered what happened to her).

The Jamboree came to an end and, on the way back home we were flat broke - not one red cent. I'll never forget, we had to change busses at Indianapolis, Indiana. It was around midnight when we arrived there and we found out that we had a layover of about 4 hours before our next bus was to depart. The bus station was right downtown so we decided to explore the city. We left our packs behind the ticket counter and started walking. Within a couple of blocks we passed a Greek restaurant from which the most wonderful aroma was escaping. We opened the door and went inside. There were a couple of customers in there and we sat down at the counter. The man behind the counter was the owner - an elderly

Greek. We ordered "glass of water". We had on our scout uniforms and after he gave us the water he started quizzing us - where you from? Where you been?, etc. Finally, he asked the magic question "want something to eat"? We told him we had no money. He rang his cash register, the drawer opened, and he handed each of us a $5 bill. Then said "now you got money - want something to eat?" In unison "Yes Sir". He served each of us a plate heaped high with a goulash, several rolls, and large glasses of milk. We were starved and the food soon disappeared - then desert appeared - Baklava - plus a milk refill. When we got ready to leave we asked for our ticket. He said "It's on the house." We thanked him profusely and gave him a hug. When we got outside we memorized the name of the restaurant and the street address.

After we returned to Dawson we presented "Programs" to all the Lions clubs in the immediate vicinity of Dawson - Princeton, Providence,, Madisonville. We concluded each with the Greek restaurant experience. Men in every audience asked for the name and address of it. There is not telling how many $5 bills Mr. Tsiropoli received in the mail and /or thank you letters. I know Rodney and I sent him one each. Things I learned in the boy scouts also had a significant influence on me for the balance of my life.

Parents encourage your children to join the scouts.

CHAPTER 16

DECEMBER 7, 1941

Things happened in the world during this period of my life that had a very major effect on me - and the world - for the rest of my life. I remember the two most significant - as if they happened yesterday.

<u>The Japanese: Attacked Pearl Harbor - Dec. 7, 1941</u>

It was an unusually mild day in west Kentucky - a Sunday. Spud Allen and I were playing "coal mining" in an earthen hill in our yard. We had trucks made from wood and had built roads on the side of the hill - and dug a hole which was the coal mine. We would load the coal (dirt) on our trucks and haul it down the hill to an imaginary town. My dad was off that day.

Suddenly, my sister Loretta, came screaming out of the house "The dam Japs have bombed Pearl Harbor." She was crying. We followed her back into the house and my mom and dad were huddled around the radio - listening to the details of the attack. They looked very solemn - my dad said "I'm going to join the Navy tomorrow" - and my mom began crying. Sis said "I wish I could get my hands on one of them damn japs - I'd scratch their eyes out." I was totally confused - I believed the japs would attack Dawson Springs by the end of the week. I asked dad "Can I borrow a quarter?" He asked "What for?" I said, "I need to get a box of 22 shells - so I can shoot some Japs." He dug in his pocket and gave me a 50¢ piece and said "Get .22 long rifle - Hollow Point!" (.22 shorts cost 25¢ a box but long rifle cost 40¢). Spud had slipped off and gone home.

For the rest of the day neighbors started coming out of their houses and gathering on the street and discussing the upcoming war. Everyone was confused - but defiant. You could detect a resolve developing - a resolve to win the war!

I'll discuss the World War II War years later - for now let's skip to the next significant event -

The U.S.A. Drops An Atomic Bomb On Hiroshima, Japan - August 6, 1945

By the time this happened, World War II had been going on for almost four years (for the U.S.), the Nazis had been defeated in Germany, and most of the war news was good. The allies were winning. The World was stunned at the destructive power of the "little boy" which we dropped on Nagasaki - killing an estimated 140,000 Japanese -mostly civilians.

In my opinion, this was the most significant event of the 20th century. From that point forward everyone realized just how precarious and uncertain life can be - and began thinking in terms of "self" rather than "we" or "us" or "nations" This led to the moral decay of the 21st Century in my view.

Back to the Chronology of my memories. I did go to O'Brien's Hardware store early on Monday morning and there was a long line (mostly men) waiting for the store to open. Most everyone in line planned to purchase the same thing - guns and ammunition. There was also a long line (mostly women) lined up at Purdy's grocery - waiting to stock up on groceries.

When wise old Mr. O'Brien got there to open his store he talked to the crowd lined up outside and explained that only 10 people could enter at a time, and that ammunition would be rationed - 1 box per customer. Everyone respected his "rules" but a few were grumbling. I was in the third group that entered the store and made my purchase of a box of Winchester .22 long rifle bullets - hollow points. Now, I was ready for the invasion - and so were most of the men in Dawson. Later that day, my dad and some of my Uncles rode the bus to Madisonville to join the Navy. Dad wasn't accepted because of his age and a hernia - but Uncle Calvin (his youngest brother) was. A sailor from Dawson (I think his name was Trotter) was killed at the Pearl Harbor bombing. After a few days, things began to sort of get back to Normal. President Roosevelt had made a stirring speech on the radio on December 8th - I remember his closing statement - "We will gain the inevitable triumph - So Help Us God."

I was only 10 when we entered the war. We got the <u>Courier Journal</u> (Published in Louisville) and I read it every day. Before long I began to understand the magnitude of the war (truly a World at War) and the weapons of war - guns, bombs, airplanes, tanks, ships and submarines. I decided to become a fighter pilot as soon as I got old enough. I read everything I could get my hands on about airplanes and flying - my favorite airplane was the Lockheed P-38 Lightning.

The major effect of World War II on the Citizens of Dawson Springs were the shortages of most everything and rationing of many food stuffs, other manufactured items, and gasoline. There was plenty of work and everyone now seemed to have money. However, after the draft began, all the able bodied men were in the service (and out of the work force) - their place was taken by the women.

CHAPTER 17

THE WAR YEARS

The years of the great war (World War II) were tough ones - particularly since I was 10 to 14 during that period and many of the things I wanted simply were not available - and many other things were rationed.

Young Men - All Gone To War

One of the most noticeable things was the lack of young men - they had all "gone to war." The next thing noticeable was - most women were now working. There was a resolve that you could feel - we were going to whip the Nazis and Japs.

News

Of course, most everything you heard on the news was "war news." During the first couple of years of the war the news was bad and people sad - but as the tide began to change - there were more smiles.

Gathering Scrap

The kids job during this great war was to gather scrap. We scrounged all over Dawson and the surrounding country side for scrap - any kind of metal. You could sell about anything metal at McGregor's scrap yard. Copper and aluminum brought the best prices.

I remember from my hunting trips where lots of trash had been dumped along roads and in ditches. Every chance I got I would go scavenging. The best finds were old miners lunch pails (aluminum) and car batteries (lead) and car generators (copper).

Plenty of Jobs

There were plenty of jobs - almost zero unemployment. However, most of the workers were either old men or 4-F or women. the coal mines were operating around the clock and there were several manufacturing plants in Evansville, Indiana where many from Dawson went to work. Dawson had a sewing plant that made uniforms. Mom got a job there - Dad, despite trying to enlist in every branch of the service, continued his job with the V.A. despite the temptation to earn much more money elsewhere.

Aunt Beadie

Arvil (Aunt Jessie's son) and Beadie (mom's sister) got married just before he entered the Army. Ermel (Aunt Jessies daughter) married Woody (Woodruff McGregor). Beadie moved out to her own little house - soon a son (Kent) was born. I spent a lot of time visiting them. Kent probably thought I was his big brother. We were a very close family

Grade School

From the 5th grade through the 8th grade I went to the "new" school building - about a mile away and closer to downtown. my next teachers were:

5th Grade - Miss Tina Luce

6th Grade - Miss Ethel Cox

7th Grade - Miss Erin Black (she emphasized spelling (in which I excelled - I won the west KY "spelling bee")

8th Grade - Mr. Tony (Mouse) (4-F) McChesney

It's amazing that, more than 50 years later, I remember my teachers. It shows how important they are - the very foundation of our society. Miss Luce drilled us on Geography - the war showed the importance of that subject. Miss Cox, a full blooded Indian, drilled us on American history and nature. Miss Black, drilled us on the arts - especially music. Mom made me take piano lessons from Miss Simons who lived about a block from us. My musical talent was absolutely zero. I never got interested and would be thinking baseball or fishing during each lesson. I barely learned the location of middle C. My dad saw what a waste of money it was - trying to teach me to play the piano - that they finally stopped the lessons. Dad would say "That boy couldn't even play a "swinette".)

CHAPTER 18

SPORTS

Basketball has always been the most popular sport in Kentucky. And Dawson was no different. Nailed to every garage and barn was a basketball net – and we played year round. The local team was the panthers, the school colors were purple and gold, and the fight son was a copy of the Notre Dame fight song. There obviously had been a very influential Catholic in the past.

At the time we were growing up, the <u>only</u> high school team was the basketball team. There had been a football team the era prior. There was a baseball team sponsored by the American Legion.

Buddy, Rod, and I played on the basketball team and Buddy and I played on the baseball team. Buddy and

Rod played the guard position and I played forward. Buddy and I both pitched and played catcher. Buddy was the best athlete of the four, followed by Rod and me and Doug just wasn't so gifted – although he later became a good golfer.

My Mother always opposed my playing sports – she insisted that I study and get a "Good" education. For that reason, I played sports on the sly – and really never put my heart into it – as did Buddy. Nevertheless, I was a good athlete.

All three of us were on the junior varsity (second) team and we won more than we lost. Only Buddy made the varsity team – Rod and I were substitutes.

Basketball as I knew it and today's basketball are very different. In my time the game was played primarily at half court with set plays – at a much slower pale. Shots beyond the free shot circle were 2 handed "set" shots – and were all for 2 points. Players were smaller – it was rare to see one over 6 feet tall and the sport was segregated. Dunk shots were unheard of. The coach insisted that free shots be shot with both hands – hold the bail at knee level and shoot under hand. Shots beyond the free throw line <u>must</u> be 2 handed set shots.

The biggest reward for playing were the bus rides home from out of town games – with the cheer leaders (particularly if you won – and more particularly if you scored a lot of points). A lot being 10 or more – the winning score was usually less than 50.

I remember one game in which the player guarding me was roughing me up pretty good but no foul was called. I lined up next to him for a free throw and told him "If you foul me one more time – I'm going to bite you." He gave me a funny look. Within a minute we were fighting for a rebound, he whacked me, and I pinched him and growled – he screeched and ran.

I remember another game in which the coach was mad at Rod and me (for shouting long range 1 hand jump shots). The out of town game was almost over an it was a close game – however, the coach had used all the other substitutes and left Rod and me warming the bench. Rod looked at me and said – "Heck fire, coach is not going to let up play. Let's go shower and get a good seat or the bus." I said "sounds good – lets go." (and we did). We had showered and were getting dressed when the coach burst into the dressing room and yelled at us – "Get back on the court or your are off my team." I already had my undershirt and shorts or so I grabbed my uniform shorts and put them on and slipped into my basketball shoes and headed for the stairs – the coach right behind me with a board. I went through the door and on to the court and immediately saw our team had only 4 players and the odd player for our opponent was dribbling toward their basket for an easy layup. I had the angle on him so I streaked out and whacked him good and he missed . He made 1 of his 2 free throws and that put them ahead by 3 points. They had an announcer who announced when I fouled "Jenkins was fouled by ….double zero of Dawson."

We called "time out" and I was able to tie my shoes and borrow a jersey from one of our team who had fouled out. Rod had taken the time to get fully dressed. When play resumed, Rod and I both were playing. He passed me the ball and I made a long one handed jump shot. Instead of racing to our half of the court on defense. Rod and I double teamed their guard and I was able to steal the ball from him and make a layup just before the buzzer sounded. We won by 1 point and I was "hero".

The trip home was spent in the back of the bus – cuddled up and smooching with a cute cheerleader. The opponents fans threw rocks at our bus as we were leaving – not uncommon in those days. Basketball was serious business in every small town in Kentucky.

Winning the state basketball championship in Kentucky was almost impossible for the smaller schools. All teams competed at the same level - no classification. Each team had to first win District, next Region, and finally State. In the case of Dawson, we could rarely get past Madisonville in the District, or if we got lucky and now, then we had Owens boro at the Region - both much larger schools. Only one time is history did Dawson make the State finals - 1946 under Paul Stevens. They made it to the State level five other times - 44, 45, 47, 50, & 55.

There are a couple of other basketball memories. In my sophomore year the coach took the team on a road tour through North and East Kentucky. We played perhaps 6 or 7 games. In the small towns, we stayed with the families of our opponents. However, The "Big" game was with the state reform school in Louisville. We stayed in the staff quarters. When we went to their gym to practice - it was full of black boys who had come to watch us.

In a room next to the gym was a boxing ring. We went over to watch a couple of them "spar". They invited us to "spar" (box). My teammates knew I had boxed some and insisted that I crawl into the ring with the black boxers - which I did with some reluctance. The young black boxer who I sparred with was very good and whipped my soundly. That night, their basketball team whipped our team even worse. I saw even then that blacks, given the chance, would dominate sports.

Baseball was different. Our "Coach" had never played the game and we had a difficult time rounding up <u>nine</u> players to field a team. Sometimes we played with only 8 - or even 7. As I said before, Buddy and I both pitched and caught. When he pitched - I caught him and vice versa. He and I practiced pitching for hours - without a coach. We learned by trial and error. Byron Gaines, the one legged shine man at the local shoe shop was an avid fan of the Saint Louis Cardinals and had played in his younger days. He taught us the various grips on the ball for a curve, fast ball, slider, and knuckle ball. My best pitches were a fast ball and overhead curve which I called a "drop" ball. Buddy's were a curve and knuckle ball.

We could hold our own against the American Legion teams from other small towns - but there weren't that many teams. Consequently, we played many local country and/or company teams. The local coal mines sponsored teams and many of the rural "cross roads" had their local team - all adults. They usually beat us with home runs.

Without properly warming up or icing down our arms - both Buddy and I had ruined them for pitching by the time we were 18.

Football was strictly sand lot variety. We couldn't even come up with 9 players for baseball - and 11 for football was out of the question. When we played football, I was the running back. My Uncles, who had played the game, told me I was good enough to play college ball. We'll never know.

I never played golf until I was in the Air Force.

Another game I learned when I worked in Michigan was badminton. Cletus Eli taught me that game and he and I won the Flint, Michigan City Champions one year.

In summary, I was a better than average athlete - without ever really applying myself. However, early in my senior year we were playing in Nebo, and there was a roof leak in their gyms it was raining and I hit a wet spot and slid into a radiator and nearly broke my hip that was the end of my playing days. Later in life I had the hip replaced.

CHAPTER 19

A TRIP THROUGH DIXIE

I have always been a joiner - and a doer. One of the organizations I joined was the FFA. (Future Farmers of America). The sponsor was the headman himself, Mr. R.A. Belt. I raised a pig and a garden for my projects. The club sold candy at school and Mr. Belt promised us that if we could save enough (he set $50.00 as our goal), he would take us on a trip as soon as the war was over and gas rationing stopped. ($50.00 was a lot of money - particularly when we sold the candy at 5¢ a bar and it cost about 3¢ a bar - when you could buy it - sugar was scarce also) we started selling popcorn and peanuts also. (Dad loaned us the popcorn popper and I raised the popcorn and peanuts in my garden - as did others.)

The big war was finally over and that summer Mr. Belt fulfilled his promise. Mr. Gentry, the Chevrolet dealer, let Mr. Belt buy the first new Chevrolet he got after the war and Mr. English loaned him a trailer. We had to pay our own expenses so we packed camping gear and loaded up for our epic journey. Our trip took us on a wide circle through the south. We crossed through east Kentucky into Virginia then the Carolinas, Georgia, North Florida, Alabama, Mississippi, Tennessee, and back to Dawson. We took turns riding in the open trailer. There were 10 of us and we would squeeze 7 in the car and 3 rode in the trailer. Each night we would find a camping spot and unload. Mr. Belt would drive to the nearest town and stay in a motel. We pitched our tents (Army Surplus Shelter Halves) and slept on the ground in Army Surplus sleeping bags. We stopped at grocery stores (usually the great A & P's or Piggly Wiggly - the first super markets) and bought food to cook and bread and bologna for lunches. We had an old kerosene lantern for light. A few times when we weren't near a state park or other convenient camping sports, Mr. Belt would stop at a farm and get permission for us to camp on the farm.

I think we must have visited every battle field of the Civil War. Mr. Belt had a great interest and knowledge of taught us as we traveled. Other points of interest that stand out in my mind about this trip were:

*The Great Smoky Mountains. *A black bear *The Atlantic Ocean. *Folly Beach, South Carolina *Savanna, Georgia *Mobile, Alabama *New Orleans, LA. *The Natchez Trace *The Parthenon (Nashville, Tenn.) *Vicksburg, Miss *Black Sharecroppers, and * Cotton Fields

I will always remember two nights in particular on that trip. The first was early during the trip and the second one late in the trip. We were gone almost a month. The first occurred when we were camped in the Smoky Mountains. A big black bear joined us - looking for food. We finally chased him off by throwing rocks and beating on pots and pans. but he scared heck out of all of us and we didn't get any more sleep that night. We were sure glad to see Mr. Belt drive up the next morning.

The next occurred late in the trip in South Mississippi. We had camped in a little patch of woods next to a large cotton field. The next morning we were awakened by the most beautiful singing I have ever heard. There must have been 3 dozen negroes in that field hoeing (chopping) cotton and signing. (I have since heard the

Mormon tabernacle choir and in my memory at least - those negroes were better).

That was one of the most memorable trips I ever took (and I've since been over most of this planet earth) and my only regret is that I did not have a camera and get pictures for posterity. None of us did.

CHAPTER 20

MISCELLANEOUS MEMORIES

The following are things I remember that didn't seem to fit elsewhere.

<u>Musical Chairs at the Churches</u>

The predominate Churches in and around Dawson Springs were the First Baptist, Methodist, Presbyterian, First Christian, Holiness (Pentecostal), and hard shell Baptist (mostly in the rural areas. Our family was First Christian (Campbellites) but most of my relative were Baptist. The one thing they all had in common was – they never kept a Preacher very long. I could never understand this. My dad told me "They were just people like all of us and sooner or later they would step on the wrong toes and get booted out." I guess.

Labor Unions – John L. Lewis

I remember adults talking and arguing about labor unions, mine strikes, etc. and about John L. Lewis – a hero of many but highly disliked by others. The strike must have been rough because I saw miners all bandaged up from fights with "scabs" and they said a couple of miners had been killed.

Wheat Harvest

Once when I visited Pa Thomas, Uncle Calvin wasn't there. They said he was off on the "Wheat Harvest". He, Uncle Stallard, and the Hale brothers had hopped a freight train and gone to Texas to work harvesting wheat. They would work their way North to Nebraska, harvesting wheat as they went. Uncle Calvin bought a Model A Ford in Nebraska and they drove back to Kentucky in it.

We Built a New House - 1939

My dad had saved enough money by 1939 to buy the materials (lumber mostly) to build our own house. He bought a lot on Keigan Street and built the house himself, with the help of Pete and Ishmael Dodge, both good carpenters who lived across the street. I was the "helper." Much of the lumber was bought from Uncle Stallards sawmill. It was a real neat 3 bedroom house with a full basement and a coal furnace – and attic fans. (The very latest in those days). We were all so proud of our new house – especially Mom. I remember Dad telling Uncle Pate that it cost $1,800 and was paid for! No more moving and darn sure – no more rent!

Jeep – Jail

Whenever we went to downtown Dawson my sister and I always visited the dime store. If we had a few cents we would buy candy – and look and wish for the toys. There was a toy jeep that I absolutely coveted. It was made of metal and had rubber wheels – and painted olive drab – just like the real thing. However, it cost 25¢ - way beyond my reach. I put it in my Santa Clause letter one year – but no jeep. My playmate, Spud Ashby got a dump truck one Christmas and we built the coal mine and road on the mound of dirt in our yard. Then, I really needed that jeep.

I slipped off one day and walked downtown and went to the dime store. I got the jeep out of the counter and rolled it around and played with it until I thought no one was looking – then I slipped it in my shirt and snuck out the door. I took it home and showed it to Spud – and we played cars all afternoon.

When my dad got home that afternoon I saw him talking to my Mother who was crying. He left and walked to town. In a while, the police chief drove up and parked in front of our house and came over to Spud and I and asked me "Where did you get that jeep?" "Found it" I lied. He said "Well, it wasn't lost – but it was reported stolen – I'm going to have to take you to jail." He picked up the jeep and got me by the arm and led me to the police car – Spud ran home and I started crying – I was scared to death.

When we got to the court house he led me back to the jail and actually locked me in a jail cell with the town drunk. I remember it smelled horrible – stale pee and old sweat. It seemed like he left me locked up for hours but it probably was less than an hour. I heard him talking to someone and in a few minutes he came and got me and took me to his office and gave me a long lecture about the law." The my dad came in and got me and we started walking home. We stopped by the dime store and I had to return the jeep and apologize for stealing it. When we got home I got more lecturing from dad capped off by a beating with his razor strap.

Except for an occasional apple, peach, or watermelon, I never ever stole anything again.

Early Disaster

Fire, flood, drowning, and cave ins – I remember one of each in particular.

The New Century Hotel Burns

The largest building in Dawson Springs was the New Century Hotel. When it caught fire, it lit up the whole sky. The fire alarm sounded for what seemed hours. I think everyone for miles around gathered to watch it burn. The fire departments from all the surrounding towns came to fight the fire. As I recall, a few hotel guests burned up in that big fire.

Flood

There was a major flood in 1937. Dawson was almost an island surrounded by flood water. I can still see all that water – you could see it from our house – it covered Highway 62.

Drowning

After the State Park and Pennyrile lakes were built - it seems like someone drowned every summer. I remember going to the State Park once and watch some men in a boat – moving around dragging grapple hooks. They finally hooked a body and rowed back to shore and drug it out on the bank. It was a young man – fully clothed. His family was crying and moaning.

Mine Cave In

There was a big cave in at the Dawson Daylight mine. We went out there with Pete and Ish. There were a couple hundred people milling around by the mine shaft – many were crying. People were trying to comfort the families of the miners trapped in the mine. We stayed until after dark – finally the rescuer crew came out – bringing the survivors – including one of my uncles. Then they reentered the mine and started removing the dead – 17 as I remember.

First Ride In A Car

The first car ride I remember was in Paul Stevens old Dodge touring car. He took all the kids in the neighbors on a ride to Charleston – and back. (about 10 miles) what a thrill!

First Airplane

Ms. Mary Emma Orr's (my first grade teacher) brother built an airplane. One day, all the school children were lead outside and watched as he flew over. Later, dad and I walked out to the farm where he kept it and I saw it up close – it looked mighty flimsy and unsafe – and it was. He later crashed and died in his flying machine.

Winter Sports

I think it snowed more in Kentucky when I was growing up than it does today. A good snow always meant a good time. We had snowman building contest, snowball fights, and made snow cream. As I got older I built a bobsled and would slide down a long hill in Dawson called Meadow Hill. One Christmas my cousins Jim and Bubbie got store bought sleds and they would let me slide down the Hill with them sometimes.

There was always a big fire built at the top of the hill and a city street ran top to bottom of the hill. At night, the street would be blocked off and after you slid down the hill, you had to pull your sled back to the top – go to the fire and warm up – then zip down again. The street lights were on and you could see ok. Some nights there would be about 50 people (kids and grownups alike) sledding on Meadows Hill.

One night I rode down with Jimmy on his sled. There was a curve at the bottom of the hill and a light pole on the outside of the curve. Jimmy was having trouble making the cure so I "bailed out". He clipped the light pole and broke his arm. The police took him to Dr. Boitnetts house who set his broken arm and put it in a cast. I felt sorry for my cousin – that ended his sledding for a couple months.

Another sport was rabbit hunting: I would take dad's .22 rifle and usually Tom Hopkins would get his older brother's .22 and go with me on a rabbit hunt. We would follow their tracks in the snow until we spotted them (you could see their ear's sticking out of the snow) or until they jumped up and ran off.

Still another winter sport when it had stayed below freezing for a couple of days was ice skating on ponds. We didn't have ice skates so I guess a better description would be ice sliding. You would back off on the bank and take a run to the ice and slide as far as you could on the ice. Hardly a winter passed that someone didn't slide too far and the ice would break and they would have to be rescued. Every pond had a couple of old boards on the bank for that purpose.

It's a wonder that we made it to adulthood – considering the risk we took as kids.

First Television

Kids, television is a relatively new thing. We didn't have a T.V. set when I was growing up. I didn't own one until after I got married. As a matter of fact, that was our first purchase.

I remember the first television set I ever saw. It was in the display window of Hayes Department Store in downtown Dawson. There was a big crowd gathered on the sidewalk and looking into the display. I wormed my way to a position where I could see what everyone was looking at and I saw a tiny movie screen (about 10 inches square) in a big box and a "movie" in black and white was playing. It appeared it was snowing wherever the movie was coming from. I asked Burr Davis what the thing was and he said "That is a television set – one of these days everybody will own one and theaters will shut down." He was half right.

Incidentally, Mr. Hayes son later became Governor of Kentucky. Congratulations Steve!

School Lunches

I remember the school lunchroom and school lunches. They cost 11¢. (It seemed that everything was a dime a penny tax back then).

After payday mom would let Sis and I buy school lunches for a few days – after that it was biscuit and bacon sandwiches in a paper sack. My favorite school lunch was shepherd's pie. (Basically browned hamburger meat stirred into mashed potatoes). If I didn't like what was served, I would walk downtown to the "Squeeze In Cafe" and get a hot dog and RC cola - 5¢ each and go by the dime store and get 1¢ worth of jelly beans (a small sack full).

Sunday School/Masonry

My parents didn't attend church regularly but Beadie usually did. She took us to Sunday school at the First Christian Church where most of my relatives attended. I joined that church when I was in my mid – teens. My Dad was a Mason and rarely missed a lodge meeting. Most of the time he was an officer. In hindsight, I think he substituted Masonry and for religion. I also joined the Masons as soon as I became old enough – 21.

After I left home, both my parents joined the church and attended regularly for which I am grateful.

I guess the reason I am a warm weather person is because the Kentucky winters were cold and the houses we lived in had grates – (people now call them fireplace) in them and were heated by coal fires. You were constantly bringing in buckets of coal and replenishing the burning coal. When you stood by the fire to warm up you burned up on one side of your body and froze on the other.

You also slept under a lot of cover (quilts and blankets). Even though I always woke up early I hated to leave the warm bed. Sometimes the house would be so cold that you could see your breath. The floors were wood or linoleum and when you stepped on them it was liked stepping on ice. (I didn't own a pair of house slippers until I was grown) it was my job to rebuild the fires in the morning.

I still hate cold weather!

First Wheels

Like most boys, I was always fascinated with wheels. Primarily, because I associated them with transportation and mobility.

The first wheels I remember were the small ones on roller skates. I got a pair of skates for Christmas when I was about 7 or 8 and soon learned to skate. I was a good skater. I would skate down the sidewalk on street to school, to Oranges Store, and later to downtown Dawson. It was a lot faster than walking.

I used to build scooters from old roller skates. They were somewhat crude – but functional. Dawson had a lot of hills and you could just fly down them. Day's Hill was close to the house.

Typical Skate Scooter

Later, I swapped a skate scooter I had built for an old wagon – and took the wheels and axles off it and built a "car"

Top View   Side View

You guided it with your feet, propulsion was provided by another kid who pushed. When you got to a hill – he would jump on and get a ride down the hill. (That was his pay for pushing you.)

(The bobsled I mentioned was this "car" with runners

replacing the wheels.)

CHAPTER 21

WHAT YOU GOT TO SWAP

I first learned about trading from Uncle Stallard, one summer when I was visited him and Aunt Alberta he took me too Princeton on First Monday. Princeton was the county seat of Caldwell county and on the First Monday of the month, the farmers met at the county fair grounds and traded (swapped as some called it). They traded everything from pocket knives to race horses – and everything in between.

A favorite trade was "pocket knives in the dark." The objective was to get the best of the trade and brag about it all day.

Sure enough, soon as we arrived a man with tobacco juice dripping down the corner of his mouth through his beard confronted my uncle and said "Stallard – want to swap knives – in the dark?" Uncle Stallard, who was an experienced trader said "Why shore Newt" and reached in his pocket and held out his fist. Newt did likewise and they each opened their fist and dropped the knives into the others hand. Newt examined his - it had a broken blade. Stallard examined his – it was missing the handle on one side. They both laughed and Newt said "a draw" Stallard nodded.

Uncle Stallard gave me the knife and said "You need to get some swapping experience – see what you can trade for today. He said "The secret to swapping is to find someone who wants whatever you've got – a lot worse than you do – and who has something to swap they really want to get and of." I started moving around the grounds – observing what people had to swap. Many of them had set up a "display" and there might be a crowd gather around – especially if the "display" contained guns or live animals (chickens, ducks, guineas, pigs, dogs (especially puppies), etc.

A fellow tapped me on the shoulder and I turned around. He was holding a purty good looking bridle but the bit was broken. He said "What you got to swap sonny?" I said "I've got a purty good bone handled Barlow knife - and pulled it out of my pocket and held it out for him to see it (good side of course). He asked "How will you swap for this race horse bridle?" I said "I'll swap my Barlow for the bridle and 10¢." He said "You got that dime on the wrong side of the trade - I'll swap the bridle for your knife and 10¢." I said "Nothing doing - and walked away." He yelled "Hey sonny - give you a nickel." I said "Deal" and we traded. He examined the knife and said "This thing ain't got the bone handle on one side" I said "I never said it did - the bit is broken on this bridle also" he said "Never said it wasn't".

I moved on through the crowd and came upon a wagon that a farmer was sitting in. There was a bushel basket full of raw peanuts in it with a homemade sign that said <u>Peanuts</u> <u>For</u> <u>Sale</u>. I asked him "How much can I get for a nickel?" He reached over and got a sack that would hold about a quart and said "This much." I handed him my nickel and he handed me the sack and said "Fill er up" and I did.

I continued wandering around - looking and eating peanuts. A man stopped me and said "I love peanuts - could I taste one? I held out the sack and said "Help yourself." He took a hand full and gave me a dime. I said "Thank you sir." He smiled and said "You're welcome sonny."

I finally bumped into Uncle Stallard and he inquired "How are you doing?" I showed him the bridle, peanuts, and dime. He said "You're going to make a trader." He showed me a 38 cal pistol and bolt action shotgun he had swapped for. He started the day with the pocket knife and a .22 rifle.

I said, I can't find anyone who is interested in this broken bit bridle. He chuckled and said "sometimes you end up with a "white elephant." However, he offered a suggestion. He suggested that I go to the area on the west side of the fairgrounds where they traded horses.

When I walked up I spotted a man holding a rope with a very nervous and jittery young horse on the other end - stomping and snorting. He saw the bridle which I had draped over my shoulder and immediately asked "What will you take for that bridle?" I'm going to need it to ride this wild horse home." I said "What you got to swap?" The rope was just looped around the horse's neck and it continued to act up - the new owner was getting desperate. He said "I'll give you that 12 gauge long Tom shotgun leaning over there on that tree (he was pointing at it). I walked over and examined the shotgun and it looked good - but I figured something was wrong with it. So I said "What's wrong with this shotgun?" He said nothing "That gun will knock a squirrel out of the tallest tree in West Kentucky." I said, "There's a box of shells by the gun - mind if I fire it?" He got even more nervous and said "Naw - you can't - it's got a broke firing pin." I said "No trade then" and started to walk off. He yelled "I'll throw in the box of shells." I continued walking, knowing I had him captured, and sure enough he yelled again "and a dollar bill". I stopped and swapped.

I looked up Uncle Stallard who said "I'm glad you are here - are you ready to leave? I said "Yes sir." He said "Stay here with this stuff while I go get the wagon" and he walked off. When he returned we loaded:

*A cage containing 20 chickens

*Another cage containing 8 pigs

*Two empty cream cans

*A cross cut saw

*His bolt action shotgun and my "Long Tom"

Riding home he asked "Did you learn anything today and what did you end up with?" I replied "Yes sir, I had fun and learned a lot - and ended up with that Long Tom shotgun, a dime, a dollar bill, and box of shells.

He said "I saw that Long Tom - purty good looking old gun." I said "It's got a broken firing pin. " He said "That's no problem, we'll take it to Calvin and he can fix it in a few minutes - makes firing pins out of nails." He said "I'm real proud of you - you did better trading than I did." I said "Thanks - but I don't think so - your shotgun looks almost new." He said "It is, but then bolt action shotguns don't work - nobody want them." I said "I know somebody that does."

We rode on awhile and Uncle Stallard finally said "Tell you what I'll do - if you will come back and help me put up my hay - I'll give you that shotgun." I said "Deal."

When I returned to Dawson I took with me a nearly new 16 gauge bolt action (with a poly choke) Mossberg shotgun, a 12 gauge, 34 inch full choke Stevens shotgun (with a new firing pin), a box of 12 gauge, No. 6 shot, shotgun shells, a dime and a dollar bill.

A few days later I approached Carroll (CT), hoping to make a trade. He was from one of the wealthier families in Dawson. His dad was a mine superintendant and his granddad was a doctor. Motor bikes were very popular - primarily because of Whizzer motors. You could install them on any bicycle. All three of my buddies had one - Doug's was brand new and Rod and Buddy had used ones. I had helped both of them fix their bikes up and had a pretty good knowledge of how the Whizzer 2 cycle gasoline engine worked.

Carol had two whizzer motor bikes - one that he had wrecked and it wasn't working and a brand new one that his granddad had bought him. He also had a neat double barrel .20 gauge shotgun that he always complained didn't shoot far enough.

When I described to Carroll what I had to swap he was very, very interested - particularly in the Long Tom. Squirrel season was about to open. I rode behind him on his new whizzer and we went by my house and looked at the guns, then took the Long Tom and a couple of shells over to his house. We got a can and were going out in a field behind his house to test the Long Tom. I told him to bring his 20 gauge also and a shell. He asked "What size?" I said #4 shot if you have one.

We sat the tin can on a fence post and paced off about 50 paces. I put the #4 shot shell in the 20 gauge "open cylinder" barrel shotgun and handed it to him and said "See if you can hit the can," he fired and missed. Then, I put a #6 shot shell in the Long Tom and handed it to him and said "Now, try this cannon." He fired and the can went flying. He was grinning from ear to ear and said "What will you take for this cannon?"

My proposition was - my two shotguns (and box of shells) for his wrecked whizzer plus his shotgun and whatever shells he had. To my amazement - he accepted - no counter offer - no argument - nothing? He even got his older sister to haul the stuff to my house in the family Buick.

I immediately started the restoration project. I took his wrecked Whizzer completely apart - piece by piece. The bicycle itself was beyond repair - for me anyway. The frame was broken in a couple of places and badly sprung - and the front wheel was badly bent. The gas tank was scratched up and had a minor dent in it, but the engine itself was in pretty good shape. I decided to go ahead and replace the piston rings, spark plug, belt, and inserts anyway while I had it broken down. there was a dealer in Madisonville that carried parts. (I asked a neighbor who went to Madisonville frequently to bring them to me.)

My bicycle was still in pretty good shape except it was scratched up badly (from the paper route use) and it needed new tires. When Mr. Ashby brought the parts - he had a surprise for me - a shiny "straight" tail pipe - chrome plated. It was brand new product and no one else in Dawson had one. It was a gift and I thanked him profusely for it.

I carefully put things back together - scavenging tires, spokes, handle bars, luggage rack, speedometer, lights, mud flaps, reflectors and sat from the wrecked bike and replacing/adding those parts to my Hawthorne. When I finally had it reassembled - it was time for the test. I put gasoline in the tank, oil in the crank case, and got on it and pedaled to the nearest hill and started down hill to get it fired up. It finally started but it was running very rough so I stopped and tinkered with the carburetor - soon I had it purring like a kitten. I rode it for a couple of hours and it was great - but I was not satisfied with its looks. It was really scratched up. I went by Hopgoods garage and asked Mr. Hopgood what he would charge to paint it for me. He studied a minute and said "If you will sand it and mask it, I'm going to be painting a car tomorrow and if you bring it by I'll squirt some paint on it for a dollar bill." I said "Deal." He gave me a couple of sheets of sandpaper and a roll of masking tape and I rode home and started getting it ready for a "paint job." Then it dawned on me - I didn't ask "what color".

When I arrived at the shop the next day, Mr. Hopgood was already spray painting a 34 Ford Coupe a beautiful maroon color. He stopped when I rode up and asked "Do you like this color - I'll be painting that pickup truck over there a jet black soon as I finish this one. I said "Maroon was one of my favorite colors." He said "Fine, get some newspapers and cover the wheels and engine and park it over there and I'll paint it in a few minutes. I did and he did. I let it dry for an hour or so and pushed it home. When I passed O'Brien's Hardware I stopped and got a small can of paint - dove gray in color.

I let it dry overnight and the next day I added the finishing touches - gray tips on the fenders and a gray stripe on the gas tank. It looked brand new and it was, in my opinion at least, the sharpest, fastest, and best sounding motor bike in Dawson. Before the gray paint had dried real good I rode it to my buddies to show it to them. Doug immediately challenged me to a race so I slipped a mothball in my gap tank (unobserved by Doug) and said "You're on - for a dollar bet." We agreed to race one time around the block - Buddy to be the judge and "Hold the money." I beat him handily and he said "Let's go again - double or nothing - my bike wasn't warmed up." I said "Ok - give Bud your $2." The next race was a little closer - but not much. He wanted to go again but I said no "I don't want to take all your money today - some other time maybe."

That day was a turning point in my youth - it gave me the "Freedom of transportation." And I've since traveled thousands and thousands of miles and seen a good part of this world.

Now that all four of us had Whizzer motor bikes, we went all over that part of West Kentucky. Those bikes cruised easily at 50 mph and probably got 100 + mpg.

One day I was cruising down the highway (near Providence) and I passed a farm house with a motorcycle parked out front and a "For Sale" sign handing on it. I turned around and rode back to look at it. The lady of the house came out and said "Want to buy it?" I said "Maybe - how much you asking?" She said "Don't know - it belongs to my boy - he went to town and should be back directly if you want to wait." I said "I'll wait a little while" She brought me a glass of lemonade and in about 10 minutes a battered old Ford pickup truck drove up and a farmer and young boy (about my age) got out. They came over and introduced themselves. The boy and I started talking trade. I soon learned that the motorcycle was a "Java" and was built in Yugoslavia. It wouldn't run and he couldn't find anyone who could fix it - they couldn't get parts.

I had tinkered with motor bikes enough that I was confident that I could fix it - using substitute parts. There were two motorcycle dealers in Hopkinsville that I had been to - each anyway, I traded my prized maroon Whizzer for that Java motorcycle that wouldn't run and the farmer agreed to haul it to my house.

As with the Whizzer, I meticulously took the Java apart, piece by piece, and cleaned each piece and checked it carefully and laid it out so I could reassemble it. I found a section of gas line that was stopped up - otherwise, everything else seemed to be fine. There were a few nicks and scratches which I straightened out, sanded, and repainted. The tires were badly worn and I replaced them. I put it back together and got it running and fine turned it. It was fine so I started riding it. Of course, it was much faster than all the Whizzer motor bikes and now all my buddies wanted a motorcycle.

I finally sold the Java to a local coal miner and started looking immediately for another bike to buy. I found one advertised in the Courier Journal. It was a Royal Enfield and the owner lived in Owensboro. He was asking about $100 more than I got from the Java. I hitch hiked to Owensboro and found the owner and checked out the bike - it ran fine. I was able to negotiate a lower price and bought it and rode it back to Dawson.

Although it wasn't necessary, I took this bike apart also and cleaned every piece and reassembled it. I also waxed and polished it. When I got it put back together it looked like a brand new motorcycle. I rode it for awhile and one day when I stopped in Hopkinsville and was putting gas into it a man walked up and asked "Would you be interested in swapping that motorcycle?" I said "Maybe - what did you have in mind?" He said that he had an older Indian Chief bike that he would trade. He worked at the station and the Indian was parked out back. It was a pretty good looking bike but showed a lot of abuse. I tried to start it - but no success. He got on it and cranked it several times before he finally got it running. (My Royal Enfield looked new - would start first try - and ran as smooth as a Singer sewing machine). After much haggling - we finally traded - even!

I added some oil and filled up the gas tank on the Indian and started back to Dawson. About a mile outside Hopkinsville I stopped and adjusted the carburetor and got it running smoother - then continued home. When I got home I decided not to take this big monster completely apart - just partially. I cleaned the filters, changed the oil, blew out the gas lines, and polished it up. The more I rode it, the better it ran, and and the easier it started. It was a <u>fast</u> machine - 100 mph was routine - the fastest I ever got was 145.

I rode that Indian for about six months - until I hit a dog one night when I was traveling at about 100 mph. I was rushed to the hospital and in a coma for about 24 hours - but had no broken bones. When I was fully recovered, I fixed up the Indian and sold it. And that was the end of my motorcycle days!

CHAPTER 22

MORE HUNTING AND FISHING

Sports, hunting, and fishing contained to top the priority list of us four musketeers until about our junior year in high school. Of course we noticed the girls and discussed dating, sex, etc. but did nothing about it. We noted that the girls in our class began to date "older" boys - boys who owned cars or had access to them. A couple of the girls even go married - and that was the furthers thing from our minds.

<u>Hunting</u>

Squirrel hunting was on the top of the list of the four musketeers. By then we had motor bikes and we would meet and ride to Newsome Hollow, the Tradewater bottoms, or a relatives farm with our rifles tied on to our bikes. When we got to the hunting area we would park the bikes, and split up for the hunt. We almost always got our limit of squirrels.

The other hunting we did was rabbit hunting. We kept the old Model A at Dog's farm and would meet there for a rabbit hunt, always at night. We would climb on the Model A and drive slowly through the pastures with carbide lights scanning in all directions - looking for shining eyes. When someone spotted eyes they would tap the driver on the shoulder and say "Stop". Everyone who saw the eyes would shoot. Usually it was a rabbit but occasionally we got a fox, or coon, or something.

We would clean the game and usually give part of it to some needy folks who we knew were "going hungry."

When Uncle Arvil returned from the war, I did a lot of quail hunting with him and his pointer - Sis. I would spend the night with them and our hunts typically began right after breakfast and ended about dark. We covered a lot of country - on foot. You had to if you expected to kill any quail - they were scarce usually.

Probably the most fun I had hunting was coon hunting with the "Old Feller" - Dick Long. He lived about 10 blocks from my family and usually kept 4 or 5 coon hounds in a dog pen behind his house. He worked in the mines and drove an old 40 Chevrolet that was dented from bumping into trees and such and the fenders rusted out. He loaded the hounds in the back seat. Typically he would pick me up about dark and we would hunt till midnight or later. Much of the time I would go to sleep in class the next day.

Fishing

Most of our fishing trips were to Pennyrile Lake. By then we each had a rod, reel, and tackle box with a fern lures. Like squirrel hunting, we would tie our stuff or our Whizzer motor bikes and ride to the fishing hole - and generally fish all day for black bass. Other favorite places to fish were the State Park Lake, Earlington Lake, The Blue Hole, and on rare occasions - Kentucky Lake. When we went to Kentucky Lake we camped out overnight.

CHAPTER 23

ZIPPING THROUGH HIGH SCHOOL

It is so strange - when I try to remember my high school days I draw a blank. I made good grades (A's & B's) and never studied. What I remember most is that I wanted to get out of Dawson, see more of the world, make some money and <u>buy a car</u>. By my senior year I found out that I had enough credits by mid-term to graduate - which I did.

My graduating class was very small - 7 girls and 5 boys. Several had dropped out - marriage or whatever.

Very early on I decided that I was going to get a college education - whatever it took. Some of the options I had were:

a. Murray State College - Murry

b. Western Kentucky University - Bowling Green

c. University of Louisville - Louisville

d. University of Kentucky - Lexington

(a) Murry State was close and inexpensive - friends of our family had a service station in Murry and told my parents they would give me a job and room and board if I came there. The negative was a very limited curriculum - they cranked out teachers and I didn't want to become a teacher.

(b) Western Kentucky University - also close and inexpensive - my Mother's Aunt Eva owned a boarding house and would provide room and board and a job. this was my second choice - cousin Jimmy Bell went there and graduated. He later worked at a bank and taught school.

(c) University of Louisville - according to mom, Dr. Jones, the local dentist would pay for my education if I became a dentist and returned to Dawson and worked for him and later bought his dental practice. I had no desire to become a dentist.

(d) University of Kentucky - This was my first choice and I would work my way through and become a geologist.

One of my teachers, Mrs. Jepson . Encouraged me to become an announcer. She thought I had a good voice and no Brogue or Twang.

My freshman and sophomore years passed rapidly - did a lot of hunting and fishing. Also, Carroll Taylor and I hitch hiked to Nashville a couple of times and went to the Grand Ole Opry. He played guitar and later went there and played with a western band.

In my junior year I finally had my first date.

And in my senior year, both Rodney and I elected to graduate at mid-term. Buddy did also and said he was going to Michigan and get a job. His Uncle, Charlie Eli, worked for General Motors and lived in Flint, Michigan. Buddy invited us to come along - and we did.

CHAPTER 24

EARLY COURTING

All four of the musketeers "discovered" girls at about the same time in our junior year. Doug was first, then Buddy, and finally Rod and I.

My high school class was very small - 7 girls and 5 boys. I always made good grades although I rarely studied. And I was always a class leader. (Just natural I guess).

None of us owned a car and our parents wouldn't allow us to drive the family car very often - except for Doug. His dad owned a new Plymouth Coupe and Doug got to drive it just about any time he wanted (he was an only child). However, it was too small for 8 so he usually went solo - or took one of us plus our date. Rodney's parent were divorced and he had no car. Buddy's dad had an old '36 Chevrolet and my dad had an old '39 Desoto.

A typical night would be - whoever had the car would pick the others up and everyone would contribute 25¢ usually and we would put a dollars worth of gas in the car (8 + gallons - gas was 12¢ a gallon then). We would drive to a neighboring town and "Cruise" the streets - trying to pick up some girls. Princeton was our most successful destination.

On those rare occasions when there was something special in Dawson (dance, party, etc.) and we all had dates with Dawson girls, we usually ended up at the Pennyville park. In the summer, we would split up and go smooch with our date but in the winter it was too cold to go outside so we would stay in the car and smooch away - and the windows would sure fog up. But that's all we ever did - just smooch - no sex.

I got lucky and met a cute girl (DRP) from Charleston who owned a new car (her parents bought it for her). It was a Chevrolet - 2 door, maroon color. It was the first new car I had ever ridden in. She liked me and we started dating steady. I liked her also - but not enough to get married, which I think is what she had in mind. The timing was just wrong so that blooming romance just faded away (I don't remember the details).

Early in my senior year I met a girl (DM) in my sisters class that I really liked. We started dating steady and fell in love. I only dated her my senior year. When I graduated at mid-term we became "unofficially" engaged (no ring). When I left to go to Michigan she promised to wait for me until I returned - then we would get married.

(I still planned to get a college degree and she planned to work to help).

There was a girl (JB) in our neighborhood who was a real tom boy. Her older brother owned a practically new basketball. Sometimes she would come to our house and bring her basketball and we would play - one on one, or "horse". In horse you had to make the same shot as your opponent - or be a horse. I usually beat her in scrimmages but she often beat me in horse. My Mom really liked her and tried to get us to date. Later when I was home from college on holidays and she was home from nursing school we had a few dates - but nothing serious. And that might have been another mistake - she was a tremendous gal. But......we just never really fell in love.

We dated practically every girl in the junior class when we became senior - and had access to <u>cars</u>. See how it worked? A car was critical if you wanted to date. Period.

CHAPTER 25

BUILDING CHEVROLETS

Right after Christmas, Rod, Buddy, and I got on a Greyhound bus and headed north - destination Flint, Michigan. Buddy had an aunt, uncle and cousin who lived there. His uncle worked for General Motors and his cousin (Cletus Ely) was comptroller at General Motors Institute. When we arrived, there was a slight problem in Flint-no jobs. Buddy and I finally landed jobs at a company that made ice cream. Rodney went to Detroit and got a job at Chrysler.

Buddy decided to return to Dawson and finish the year in school - he found out that he was 4 credits short and hadn't graduated as had Rod and I. I rented a room from a young couple from Pine Bluff, Arkansas (Calvin and

Susan). I figured I had worn out my welcome at Buddy's relatives. It was a lucky move - Calvin worked at the Chevrolet Assembly Plant and helped me get a job there. It was walking distance from their house. The only thing I didn't much like was that I had to join the union. (They deducted the union dues from your pay check.)

I was true blue to Doris and wrote her everyday - and she did the same. I would reread her letters as I lay in bed at night - then fall asleep and dream of her. The Ely's stayed in contact and frequently invited me to dinner at their home. Cletus belonged to a health/sports club and he took me there occasionally. He played badminton and taught me to play. He and I won the championship at his club.

The only thing I was interest in was working and saving money - for a wedding and for college. My first job on the Chevrolet assembly line was installing brakes. I worked hard and fast and volunteered for overtime and extra shifts at every opportunity. My hard work was noticed and they trained me to be a "utility man." Basically, I learned to do all the jobs on a section of the assembly line and filled in for anyone absent or became a "relief man." This allowed me to work as often and as long as I wanted.

I got along fine with all the workers - about 90% of which were from the south - particularly KY, Tenn., Ark, Ala, GA, Miss. The union steward (Larkin McFatrick was from Georgia). He looked out for me - a hillbilly.

My closet friend at work was Eddie. He was from Owosso, Michigan and his family still owned a large farm there. He and his new bride took me to the farm several times. We fished in their small lake and hunted pheasant in the winter. I remember one trip when the snow was so deep that snow plows had piled it so high it was like driving through a tunnel.

I remember another trip that Cletus and I took to the upper Peninsula to watch ski jumpers compete (at Iron Mountain). I wanted to try a ski jump but Cletus strongly advised against it.

I became a workaholic and, except for an occasional trip to fish or hunt, that's all I did. Calvin and Susan had a baby and I also did some babysitting - and wrote letters. Finally, the day came when I didn't receive a letter from Doris. I didn't receive a letter from her for a week. Then she wrote a "Dear John" and enclosed a newspaper clipping with her wedding announcement. (she married a soldier from Fort Campbell.)

My dreams came to an end. I was absolutely heartbroken. I started working double and triple shifts - and drinking. Calvin and Susan, Eddie, and the Ely's all detected the change in me and tried to cheer me up. Susan tried to line me up with blind dates, as did Eddy's wife. Cletus tried to get me to apply at General Motors Institute and make a career with General Motors. He knew I had a couple of small scholarships and had already applied and been accepted at the University of Kentucky.

But it was Eddy who finally brought me out of my trance. He invited me to a <u>Polish</u> wedding (he was Polish). I accepted and went with him and his bride to the wedding in Owosso. It started on Friday and ended on Monday morning. I drank, danced, ate, danced, drank, and smooched with all the beautiful Polish girls for a whole weekend. He and I both had terrific hangovers on Monday but somehow made it to work.

Eddy's wife arranged for me to spend a fishing weekend at Houghton Lake. The girl she paired me up with had wealthy parents who owned a large lake house and boat on the lake. Eddie and wife came along as chaperones. I caught a large Muskie and nearly got caught myself - she proposed to me! And I <u>almost</u> accepted - but didn't.

I finally let Cletus talk me into applying at General Motors Institute of Technology. It was a Co-op Program and the plant where I worked sponsored me. However, I had waited until the summer was over to apply and it was time to head back to Kentucky if I was going to make the fall semester at UK.

So I packed up and said goodbye to Michigan and rode the Greyhound south.

CHAPTER 26

GO WILDCATS!

When I got back to Dawson - everything had changed. My sister was married, Rodney had joined the Marine Corp, Buddy had joined the Navy, Doug had moved to Lexington and was going to enroll at UK, my cousin Jimmy had moved to Bowling Green and applied at Western KY - and I've already told you about my ex finance. In addition, Joyce, the neighbor was in nurses school in Louisville, and Dora, the new car girl, was married. There was a registered letter waiting for me - from General Motors Institute. I had been accepted. I thought it over carefully and finally decided that the University of Kentucky was for me. I wrote GM Tech and and declined. Was that a mistake? My world had changed drastically. It was about to change again.

I was only there a couple of days - just long enough to pack - up and get ready for my trip to Lexington. Dad let me borrow the old Chevy to haul my possessions to my new home. It seem like a long trip (maybe 200 miles) (after I lived in Texas a while the "Long" trips back east were laughable.)

When I got to Lexington I called Doug (he was staying with a cousin) and he met me and led me to the campus. I got a room at the dorm and unpacked my stuff - and the next day was registration. It took a while to get readjusted. It was quite a change from working the Chevrolet plant - actually much easier. It took me a while to realize I would need to study if I was to make good grades in college - and it was strictly up to me.

There was no one there to prod me. Tom Hopkins, a childhood friend was a sophomore and he was a big help in getting me started on the right path in college.

Fortunately, money was no problem - for a change. I left Michigan with a money belt around my waist containing almost $2,000 which I had saved. I knew I couldn't get through college on $2,000 but I planned to work also. After I got settled in good I started looking for a part time job. And I ended up with several - as follows:

1. Working at a Gulf Service Station in the ritzy part of Lexington on the weekends (after a year I managed the station for George Smith - the owner) I think I started at 75¢ an hour and ended at $35.00 per weekend. (Plus tips - which were sometimes more than my paycheck).

2. Salad Chef at the Lafayette Hotel (High Class Hotel in Lexington) - token salary but got all my meals free - no limit on menu.

3. Para mutual clerk at Keenland Race Track - just during racing season. (about $1 per hour - plus winnings - minus losses)

4. Tutor (for athletes) - I think I made 75¢ an hour for this (but I studied as I taught - not a bad deal)

4a. Auditor (for fraternities and sororities) - I worked for the dean of students and audited the financial reports submitted by the social fraternities and sororities - at 75¢ an hour.

5. Dorm monitor - a dorm policeman - more or less - reported to dean of men students - no pay but got my room free.

6. Loan Shark - I would loan $4 for repayment of $5 within a week.

7. Fast food business - got a small refrigerator and kept cokes in it - made sandwiches, packaged them and kept them in refrigerator - sold a sandwich and a coke for 25¢ (cost - excluding my labor - about 10¢).

In addition, I enrolled in The Reserve Officers Training Corps (ROTC) and received, as I remember, about $75 a month. After I got the convertible, I would rent it for $10 a night.

My grades were good – about A – B+ average. I was elected to the Accounting Honorary Society – Beta Alpha PSI. Getting ahead of the story, but when I graduated I owned a new Mercury and had about $5,000 in the bank – plus a degree with a dual major - accounting/geology and a much valued job.

The job at the service station was my favorite. After my work in the car factory I know quite a bit about cars. The station was located in the "rich folks" neighborhood and most of the customers were wealthy (and most were old women). I always checked their cars thoroughly (air, oil, cleaned windshield, swept inside, etc.) and they nearly always gave me a tip - .50¢, $1 and up. I also smiled a lot and bragged on their Cadillac's, Lincoln's, Rolls Royce's, etc. When they brought them in for service, I always washed them. I talked Georgia into buying a washing machine and dryer and a supply of bath towels so we could dry them off. He also sprung for a buffer and stock of windex. We then started polishing cars. The business grew – and prospered. I worked hard at it.

I rode the bus to work and after a few months George met me at the door after I got off the bus and said – Willie, I've got something for you. He handed me a set of car keys and led me to the back of the station. There sat a 1939 Ford convertible – it was dark (Forest) Green in color and had a few dents, slick tires, and a worn out top. He said, it's all yours and you can buy whatever you need to fix it up – and I'll pay for it. Now you can get to work sooner and stay later. And I did.

For the next couple of months I spent every spare minute working on that Ford. I ordered a new top, seat covers, rings, valves, etc. One of the workers at the station (Elmer – from the East Kentucky Mountain) was a good "body man" and he took care of the dents, etc. We pulled the engine and cleaned it and completely rebuilt it. I installed a new top and seat covers and put a new set of tires on it – snow grips on the rear. When we were finished it was almost a new car – and very sharp looking - and fast! Of course, it had UK and Wildcat decals on every window – and I almost forgot dual tailpipes and a deep throated muffler. It would really peel rubber.

Some of the things I noticed very early about college were as follows:

*The opportunity to learn was there – but it was up to you to take advantage of it

*There was a noticeable diversity of subjects.

*There was a noticeable diversity of backgrounds In the student body – thus a vast diversity in motivations.

*The professors did not always stick to the subject – in a math class for example the profession might spend the

entire class time discussions a world event, a movie he saw, a book he read, etc., etc. – anything but math.

*If you expected to get good grades - you had to study <u>on your own</u>!

After the newness wore off – you fell into a routine and mine was somewhat as follows:

*All my life I have been an early riser so I tried to schedule early classes whenever possible (nearly always possible since most students liked to sleep in).

*Avoid Saturday classes because I worked that day.

*Do my studying late, late – after things settled down at the dorm.

*Play poker as much as possible.

*Join every "bull session" – and <u>contribute</u>.

A typical day for me would be as follows:

1. Rise at 6:00 a.m.- shave and shower – stop by the donut shop for donuts (5¢ each) an coffee (5¢) and have a couple of donuts (the best I've ever eaten – cake with icing) and coffee – then walk to my first class (usually at 8:00a.m.).
2. Go to classes all morning – if there was a break – go to the student union and study (or prepare for a tutoring session if I had one scheduled that afternoon).
3. When classes were over – go to grocery store and get supplies – then to my room and fix sandwiches. (eat lunch – sandwich usually).
4. Take a nap till about 5 p.m.
5. Go to the hotel and prep salads – pull lettuce, clean and chop tomatoes, carrots, radishes, etc. – store

them in buckets in the cooler. Then make up the salads for the evening meal.

6. Eat a delicious meal prepared especially for me. (steak, chicken, roast, pheasant, quail, etc. etc.

7. Back to the dorm –

*Tutoring session – sometimes – with a thick skulled football player most of the time.

*Join a bull session or poker game.

*Serious studying from around 12:00 pm to 3:00 or 4:00 a.m.

* Then sleep a couple of hours.

Most of my courting was late dates during the weekend - Saturday night and/or Sunday night. Usually to a movie – or dinner at The Lafayette Hotel – or something on the campus (plays, concerts, etc.). The expectation was sporting events - students got in free so I always took a student date to them. The University of Kentucky won nearly all of its home games – basketball and football. I didn't realize at the time but U.K. was at the peak of success with Adolph ("The Baron") Rupp coaching basketball and Paul (the "Bear") Bryant coaching football. At one time or another I had tutored most of the players and had visited several times with both coaches (concerning players with academic problems.) My dates were always impressed when a player or coach would yell or wave at me.

In addition to Doug and Tom (from Dawson Springs), my new found friends were Al, Frank, Sam, Bill, Frank F., Marvin, Ted, Tom S., and Steve. The first four were military veterans attending school under the GI Bill. Al and Frank were from West Virginia, Sam from Cynthiana, and Bill from Louisville. Frank F. was from

Peekskill NY and Marvin from Brooklyn. Ted was from Fort Knox, Tom S. from Richmond, and Steve from Dixon, Kentucky. This diversity of backgrounds resulted in some very interesting discussions.

Al (short for Almer) was from a poor coal mining family in West Virginia. He was one of the most intelligent men I ever knew. He had joined the Navy at age 16 and became a Navy Seal. During the war (WWII), he parachuted into China with a radio and was a spy. He radioed his reports to a sub stationed off shore and lived by his "wits." The Communist were taking over China and he had to avoid capture by them. He finally finished his mission, was picked up by a sub, and returned to the U.S.A.

He was working on a masters degree in engineering (when he graduated he returned to West Virginia –

married a mine owners daughter, and became quite wealthy when the owner died and the daughter inherited the mine.

Frank was married and had a couple of kids. HE was a professor at Marshall University and was on a leave of absence and getting his PHD in economics. He returned to Marshall and became a dean.

Sam was studying accounting and working on his B.S. degree. He graduated and went to work for a firm in Louisville. He was a vet from the Army. I helped him with his studies.

Bill was also an Army vet (green beret). He had recently returned from the war in Korea and was very near a psycho. He was large, strong, and mean – and not too sharp. He loved to fight and I went to a bar with him one night. And nearly got killed when he started a fight with 3 local toughs, I never knew what happened to him – he dropped out of school.

Frank P., was an Italian boy from Peekskill NY. He invited me to his home during a semester break and it turned out to be very impressive – a large mansion in fact. I never knew for sure but I always suspected his folks had something to do with the mafia. Frank never discussed them.

Marvin was a character. He was Jewish and a psychology major. He grew up in Brooklyn and it showed. He loved to argue – about anything. I often wondered whatever happened to him. HE was still in school when I left – working on his PHD.

Tom P. was another character – and an alcoholic. He was from a wealthy family and drove a new Plymouth Sedan. He literally lived on beer - he consumed a case each and every day! His favorite pass time was driving to Berea for supper. Several of us went with him on a few trips. He was also a great practical joker.

Something we would drive south to Berea, Kentucky for dinner at Berea College. Berea College was for students from poor mountain families in East Kentucky. The students literally ran the college – the food they prepared was excellent and inexpensive. I always had a lot of respect and admiration for Berea.

Sometimes, we would spend the weekend, just traveling around East Kentucky and east Tennessee. It was beautiful scenery but the natives were obviously very poor.

And Doug's cousin, who lived in nearby Richmond, owned an airplane – a Cesena. Doug and I would go visit him and he taught us how to fly the Cessna.

Stan was from Dixon (not too far from Dawson Springs) and a freshman like myself. He had a Chevrolet station wagon and during holiday and semester breaks would drive home. All of us from that area would ride home with him – we paid for the gas. (about 75¢ each) I usually rode in the very back (3 row) seat with a cute little gal from Beaver Dam and we would hide under a blanket and smooch all the way.

During the break between my freshman and sophomore year, my cousin Jimmy Bell, and I went to Wisconsin and worked for LeSeur Canning Co., canning peas and corn.

CHAPTER 27

DECISIONS, DECISIONS, DECISIONS

After my first freshman semester, I began taking 20 credit hours per semester – and auditing other classes as time permitted. Why? I wanted to learn – about everything – and I wanted to get my money's worth while I was there.

Between my sophomore and junior year I drove a truck for a construction company out of Memphis, Tenn. who was rebuilding the road from Dawson to Hoptown (Hopkinsville). I think they paid $1 per hour. The good thing was I could stay at home and save money.

When I registered for my junior year it was decision time. Like most, I really wasn't sure what I should select for a major. I got too much conflicting advice and I was interested in too many thing. I finally decided that I wanted to be a geologist. (Remember Mr. Voories – Chapter 6). So I loaded up on geology courses. When classes began they were packed – mostly with the older GI's.

I met a cute blonde (LT) from Erlanger, KY late in my junior year and we started dating. Before I realized it we were getting serious. She was a year behind me and stayed in school that summer to "catch up". I stayed in Lexington and took a couple of courses but worked most of time – running the Gulf station.

I don't recall the details but during the first semester of my senior year I discovered there was a "surplus" of geology graduates and most of them were not finding jobs, I discussed the situation, particularly with Al and Frank, and they advised me to change my major. I did a lot of research and found there was a strong demand for accounting majors – and a relatively short supply of accounting graduates. I had already taken a couple of accounting classes and made good grades in them – so I switched to accounting as my major. (I remember Cletus Ely trying to get me to go to General Motors tech and become an accountant – like himself – Chapter 10)

Sure enough, when the recruiters showed up the next spring, there were many looking for accountants, but another problem arose. The Korean war was raging and every able bodied male taking ROTC was being called to active duty almost immediately upon graduating. And I had continued Air Force ROTC throughout.

I went to a couple of interviews with major accounting firms (Big 8) and was told "we would offer you a job –

except for the ROTC problem – come see us <u>after</u> you get out of the service."

I decided the job interview were a waste of time and didn't sign up for any more. I decided that I would go home after I graduated, get some kind of job, and await my call to active duty in the Air Force . (Lucy, my girlfriend wanted me to stay in Lexington and for us to get married).

About that time, there was an ad in the campus newspaper "New Mercury For Sale" – the price was cheap and I had the money – so I bought it and sold my Ford convertible. The seller had received his orders to report to active duty and he really didn't like the Mercury which a wealthy grandparent had given him for a graduation present. He wanted a Buick.

There were about two weeks of classes left my senior year when my favorite accounting professor, Russell O'Grady, asked me to stay after a class – which I did. He told me a partner from one of the Big 8 accounting firms (Haskins & Sells) was there in the building and wanted to interview me. He explained that the partner, Mr. Charles Swarmstead, had been ill and unable to come to the campus during the scheduled recruiting period (Feb) and had gotten special permission to come late (May). He had reviewed the files and only wanted to interview me and a fellow student – Sydney!

I told professor O'Grady that it was a waste of time – he would tell me to come to see him <u>after</u> I finished my military commitment. Professor O'Grady said "Not so – I think he really wants to hire you." So I finally gave in and followed him down the hall and into the office occupied by Mr. Swormstead. After introducing us, he left.

Mr. Swormstead gave me some literature and a "Sales Pitch." I finally interrupted him and said "Sir, I don't want to sound disrespectful but I've been through this with other recruiters and I know where you are heading. So, let's not waste each other's time – go ahead and tell me to come see you after I get out of the Air Force." With that I arose and headed for the door. He nearly shouted "Mr. Thomas, would you like to work for Haskin's & Sells – now? "Heck yes" I responded. He said, "Report to my office as soon as you can – the address (Cincinnati office) is in the Brochure." I said "Yes Sir, I'll be there two weeks from Monday."

My folks came up for graduation and when that was over, I packed my possessions in the new Mercury and

Lucy and I, who were engaged by then, headed for Erlanger, KY (her hometown – across the Ohio river from Cincinnati). I had already met her parents on a previous visit and was somewhat familiar with the territory. I got an apartment near the airport and Lucy helped me get unpacked and settled in. Then we went to her parents for a big dinner and meeting with a bunch more of her relatives.

On Sunday afternoon Lucy and I drove across the river (Ohio) to Cincinnati and located the Haskins & Sells (H&S) office, parking lots, etc. so that I could find my way around on Monday morning.

On Monday morning I drove to Cincinnati and reported for work at H&S and Lucy headed back to U.K. for summer school. At H&S I was given a tour of the offices, filled out a bunch of forms, and was handed an airline ticket and expense check and told to be in the New York office the next morning for the indoctrination program. So I drove back to my apartment, packed, slept, and got a cab to the airport Tuesday morning.

The next ninety days were days of "wonderment" in the "big apple" for a country boy like me. There were about 100 new recruits in our class – from all over the USA. We were housed at the Engineering Club on 42nd Street – Very near the center of Manhattan. The H&S office was on Wall Street. In a very short time we learned how to use the subways and the streets layout was squared with avenues running one way and street another (and most numbered – easy to learn).

We would attend classes part of the time and get "on the job" training (actually working in corporate offices of major public companies – those I remember working in were RJ Reynolds Tobacco Co., Lowes Hotels, Merrill, Lynch, Fenner & Smith and 3M. We had many meetings, parties, etc. – it was great. We all thought we were really hot stuff. New York partners would take us out at night – plays, dinner, bars, etc. My roommate, Harvey Saari from Montana, and I could hold our liquor better than most and one of the senior partners apparently enjoyed going out on the town with us. One night, we stayed out all night and spent from around 1:00 a.m. to sun up in a small bar (in Greenwich Village). We entertained the small crowd – Harvey played a guitar and sang cowboy songs – and the partner and I joined in on the chorus – and I told dirty jokes.

We were not smart enough to figure out that they were "evaluating us." Whoever took you out completed a questionnaire the next day and it went into your personnel file. Sort of chicken sh….. don't you think.

After a month or six weeks, Manhattan started to get old. By then we had seen most of the tourist attractions (Empire State, Coney Island, boat trips, of Liberty, Museums, Broadway shows, etc.). So, on weekends a few of us would hop on the train on the weekends and go to Connecticut, New Jersey, Pennsylvania, etc.

For the first month or so I got a letter from Lucy every day – then they started to slack off. Oh no, though I – here we go again. Sure enough, I finally got a letter saying she was very lonely and had agreed to go to a fraternity dance with a boy she had dated before she met me.

Ok thought I – two can play that game. I had met a real cute girl in one of the offices where I had worked so

I had an opportunity to go back to that office and look her up and ask her out. She accepted and gave me her address. On the night of the date I took a cab to pick her up – at a mansion on the Hudson river. A butler answered the door and she came down decked out in a mink coat and diamonds. Her father was <u>very</u> wealthy.

We had dinner at the Waldorf Astonia and then danced to the Sammy Kaye orchestra in the Blue Room. Fortunately, I had cashed my paycheck that afternoon (around $400) but by the time I paid up and got her home – I barely had enough to pay the cab. The cabbie recognized my situation and gave me a free ride back to the Engineers Club. (in those days – New York city was a safe city and the New Yorkers were nice people – not the case in later years when I returned).

I was flat broke so Harvey loaned me $10. H&S always furnished lunch and dinner at most of the functions. For breakfast I would grab an orange slush and a hot dog from a street vendor (25¢) and at night I would get a chicken pot pie at a Horn and Hardart. Whenever I got the chance, I would sneak a sandwich, apple, etc. from one of the H&S supplied meals. The moral of this story is – be very careful about who you ask out on the date in New York.

The "indoctrination" program was completed by about the first of September and at our "graduation" they gave out some silly awards. Harvey and I won the entertainment award and had to get up before the group and sing a western son (guitar provided). Harvey selected "Get along little doggies". The partner (Sorry –

forgot his name) joined us and we got a big round of applause. I then told a couple of jokes.

Later in the program I was awarded "Best candidate for dictator" award. At one training session conducted by some psychiatrist we had been split up into teams of ten and given a complex problem to solve. After my team struggled with it for a few minutes I took charge and split our group up into teams of 3, gave each team a segment of the problem, made them write their solution, then put it all together and presented our answer. We finished first and had the right answer. (Done just like Adolph would have handled it.).

CHAPTER 28

OFF WE GO - INTO THE WILD BLUE YONDER

When I reported back to the Cincinnati Office, Mr. Swarmstead called me into his office and patted me on the back and said "we got a very good report on you from New York – stick with us and you will go far with H&S." And I did – stick with them that is – for too darn long. (I never learned the game of "politics" in a big firm).

The first weekend back I drove to Lexington to see Lucy. She had joined a Sorority and was having a grand ole time – party after party. She didn't respond when I kissed her and finally got up enough courage to give me the engagement ring back and break our engagement. I was heartbroken – again! But not as much as the first time. She had put on some weight. (I later learned that she got married the next week and seven months later had a baby girl – <u>not</u> mine!)

Since I was foot loose and fancy free I volunteered for "out of town" duty and literally spent the next three months traveling all over Ohio, Indian, Kentucky, and West Virginia. I lived out of my Mercury and rarely went back to my apartment in Erlanger. Most of the time I was a member of an audit team headed by a "senior accountant" and doing "grunt" work – cash balances, transaction tests, counting inventory, etc. But I learned fast and started doing some small audits (brokerage, utility sub offices, auto dealerships, etc.) by myself. One of my mentors, Will West, taught me a lot about auditing and I'll always be in his debt, Cliff did too as did Jerry Diehl.

Mr. Jerry Diehl had been a partner in the Manila, Philippine Island office in 1941 when the big war began and had been captured by the Japanese and held in a concentration camp throughout the war. No doubt he had suffered many atrocities from the Japanese. He was spending the last couple of years in the Cincinnati office, operating as a senior accountant, before retirement. He was strictly "old school" and I had to pack and carry the work bags, wear a hat, and walk 3 paces behind him – and also chauffeur him around.

On one of the earlier audits I uncovered a major fraud. It was almost by accident and when I showed what I had found to the senior accountant, he immediately called the Cincinnati office and a much more experience crew (including 3 partners) arrived the next morning and we were sent to another audit. I later heard that the perpetuator of the crime had fled to South America and the total theft was about $3 million. I thought – "Gee, this is going to be an exciting profession."

During this period it was all work and no play. We were not allowed the fraternize with the clients employees and they were the only girls I met – I was constantly traveling. I did have a couple of "blind dates" which clients had arranged – but they were duds, for entertainment we went to movies, ball games, and I read and studied for the CPA exam.

Around Thanksgiving I received a letter from my Uncle Sam. He ordered me to report to active duty at Lackland AFB, San Antonio, Texas on January 4th. A career change was immediately ahead.

Right before Christmas I "processed out " at H&S - Cincinnati and went on a "military leave of absence." I packed up and checked out of my apartment and drove to Dawson Springs for the Christmas Holidays. It was cold and snow was on the ground.

I spent the Christmas Holidays with my folks and did some quail hunting with Uncle Arvil. On January 2, I packed one again, climbed into my Mercury, and headed for Texas. I'll always remember that day – cold and snowing – hard. I was all bundled up in heavy clothes. I drove through Tennessee, Mississippi, and Louisiana (spent the night in Jackson, Mississippi).

One thing I noticed immediately was an improvement in the weather and temperature as I moved southward. I started shedding those heavy clothes.

Before heading to Texas I had sold my '39 Ford convertible and bought a practically new black Mercury 2 door sedan. It had a large V8 engine and overdrive – a very fast car. So I drove into Texas in a practically new fast car that was paid for and had several hundreds of dollars in travelers checks.

My first exposure to Texas was at <u>Waskom</u>. I stopped at a restaurant and had a <u>Texas</u> breakfast – steak and eggs. Everyone was in short sleeves and the sun was shining bright. I've always been a warm weather person and I thought – this is the place for me – I'm never going to leave Texas!

And I didn't!

The End of this book.*

*Military experience is covered in my next book – "I Smell Smoke." Then, my professional career to present follows in "The Debits Are On The Left, The Credits Are By The Window."

BOOKS WRITTEN BY
BILL R. THOMAS

Title	Brief Description
1) A Summer on Piney Creek	A Summer Spent with Friend Living in a Cave on Piney Creek (Kentucky)
2) Hickory Fired Tobacco, Moonshine Whiskey, Beautiful Horses, and Fast Women	Kentucky Based Short Stories
3) Bill T's Texas Bob Tales	Texas Based Short Stories
4) I Smell Smoke	Authors Experience as B-47 Crew Member in Strategic Air Command
5) My Most Memorable Adventures - One Hunting and One Fishing	Hunting Trip in Mexico and Fishing Trip in Alaska
6) The Accumulated Wisdom of the Bugscuffle Domino, Whittle and Spit Club	Philosophy and Wisdom Gained Over a Colorful Lifetime
7) The T-Bone Ranch	Developing a Cattle Ranch in Montague County, Texas
8) A Wild Shot In The Dark	Autobiography - Birth Through Air Force
9) The Debits Are On The Left, The Credits Are By The Window	Autobiography - Air Force to Present

Books may be purchased at - Lulu.com (Bill's Books)

www.ingramcontent.com/pod-product-compliance
Lightning Source LLC
Chambersburg PA
CBHW032036150426
43194CB00006B/302